COACHING

For Dean and Wendell,
colleagues in learning and life

COACHING

WINNING STRATEGIES FOR INDIVIDUALS AND TEAMS

DENNIS C. KINLAW

Gower

Published by
Gower Publishing Limited
Gower House
Croft Road
Aldershot
Hampshire GU11 3HR
England

Gower
Old Post Road
Brookfield
Vermont 05036
USA

Dennis Kinlaw has asserted his right under the Copyright, Designs and Patents Act 1988 to be identified as the author of this work.

British Library Cataloguing in Publication Data
Kinlaw, D. C. (Dennis C.)
    Coaching : achieving continuous development with
    individuals and teams
    1. Leadership   2. Employees – Training of
    I. Title
    658.3'124

ISBN 0 566 07888 0

Library of Congress Cataloging-in-Publication Data
Kinlaw, Dennis C.
    Coaching : achieving continuous development with individuals and
    teams / Dennis C. Kinlaw
        p.   cm.
    Includes bibliographical references and index.
    ISBN 0–566–07888–0 (cloth)
    1. Personal management.   2. Employees – Training of.   3. Employee
    motivation.   4. Work groups – Management. I. Title.
    HF5549.K497   1997
    658.3'1245–dc21   96–37781
                                                                 CIP

Typeset in Century Schoolbook by Poole Typesetting (Wessex) Limited and printed in Great Britain by Biddles Ltd., Guildford.

CONTENTS

LIST OF FIGURES

PREFACE

The first premise of this book is that coaching is one of the most useful functions that any leader can practise to create winning performance in individuals and teams. The second premise is that everyone is a leader at one time or another and everyone needs to know how to be a successful coach.

Coaching has been recognized as a useful leadership function for as long as individuals have been helping each other solve performance problems, teach each other new knowledge and skills, challenge each other to reach for ever higher levels of performance, and confront each other to improve performance. Today, however, coaching has become not merely a *useful* leadership function, but a *critical* leadership function.

Organizations will remain competitive to the degree that they fully use the mental resources which are available to them. Developing competent people and ensuring that those people have the opportunity to exert competent influence from top to bottom in an organization are the keys to making full use of an organization's mental resources.

Coaching develops competent people and extends their influence. It gives people new knowledge and skills, new confidence and new commitment. It removes performance obstacles, and challenges and resolves performance problems.

Organizations have learned that it is expensive and wasteful to maintain the layers of management that have existed in the past. The elimination of managers and supervisors, the growth of self-managed teams, and the empowerment of every worker require that leaders spend more and more time developing people and less and less time trying to control them.

Coaching is a proven and powerful strategy for developing people. It creates winning performance by creating people who are clear about what is important, who are competent to do their jobs, who have the confidence to carry out difficult tasks, who take control over their own performance and who are committed to do their very best all of the time.

Coaching rests upon the simple belief that individuals and teams want to win. They never want to fail. They always want to do their best and be perceived as doing their best. Coaching transforms these desires and expectations into the practical winning outcomes of customer satisfaction and the continuous improvement of the processes and conditions that produce customer satisfaction.

In writing this book, I am indebted to the thousands of people who have used what I have written in the past about coaching and by whom I have been stimulated to expand my own thinking about coaching and to extend my understanding of what coaching in organizations is and what it can do. I am also most appreciative of the many people who have participated in my coaching training workshops over a period of 30 years and who have demonstrated time and again that coaching is something that everyone can learn to do. These many people have confirmed to me repeatedly that there is no greater direct and personal contribution that we can make to ourselves, our teams, and our total organizations than by coaching our co-workers, our teams and our whole organizations to win.

Finally, I should like to thank my wife, Stella, for her help in reading this book as it took shape and for putting the final manuscript into a state for the publisher.

Dennis C. Kinlaw

INTRODUCTION

At the beginning of a series of leadership training programmes that I delivered for many years for various engineering and scientific organizations, I asked the participants this question: 'All of you have enjoyed considerable success in this organization. How do you account for your success?'

As might be expected, I was given many answers. Some admitted (with various degrees of reluctance) to being bright and hard-working. Some allowed that they had enjoyed a fair amount of luck by just happening to be 'the right person around when a new opportunity appeared'. Some mentioned their specific strengths, such as giving attention to detail, being willing to do the dirty jobs, getting along with people and the like. There was, however, one answer which was included in the responses of most of the participants. Most of them acknowledged a debt to one or more persons who had helped them.

When I further asked participants to give specific examples of who had helped them and how, they described various managers, project managers, supervisors, team leaders, and co-workers who had *personally* assisted them to:

O   learn some new skill
O   resolve some technical or organizational problem
O   balance some personal problem with the demands of their job
O   understand the expectations of higher management
O   take the risk of some more difficult responsibility
O   separate what was more important from what was less important
O   become better organized

○   understand the unwritten rules
○   learn how to help others achieve
○   learn how to gain the commitment of others
○   know when to stop advocating and start cooperating
○   develop themselves with others into a high-performance team and so on.

What these participants were describing when they specified the kind of help which they had received was the help of being coached. Over the years, I have catalogued hundreds of comments that people have made in accounting for their own successful performance. Most of these have included some reference to one or more persons who were their coaches. These comments describe more than facts. They describe a sense of profound debt and appreciation. Here are some examples:

> Whatever understanding I have about leading an organization, I owe to him. This is something I can never repay. I only hope that I can pass what I learned from him on to others.

> Sometimes I find myself not only expressing the ideas that she gave me, I hear myself actually using her words.

> I was at a real impasse at the time. The project was going down the tubes and I had no one to blame but myself. I just had not taken the time to build a team and get everyone's full commitment to what we were doing. Thank goodness I had enough courage or smarts to go ask a fellow project manager of mine for help. There is no way to put a price on what he did for me. He saved my project and my career.

> What I remember about my boss was that he just seemed to live what he said. He was the personification of wisdom and sound judgment. He will always be the embodiment for me of the leader who can be tough, yet compassionate. He was never too busy to answer my questions, to help me solve some problem, to give me feedback and show me how to improve.

This book has been written with the firm conviction that:

1. coaching has been one of the most pervasive and success-
    ful functions performed by people at all levels of every
    organization; and
2. coaching accounts in considerable measure for people's
    success in their organizations.

Find an organization in which competencies are easily
shared and developed and you will find an organization in
which coaching of the less skilled by the more skilled is pervasive and routine. Find an organization in which there is full
congruence between the organization's core values and the
behaviours of its people, and you will find a multitude of
instances where leaders are taking time to indoctrinate new
members in these values and to clarify these values with their
co-workers. Find an organization in which team development
and team performance have really taken hold and teams are
fulfilling everyone's expectations and you will find an organization in which team leaders spend much of their time coaching
their teams. Find an organization which has a culture that fully
supports innovation, risk-taking, and personal initiative and
you will find an organization in which hundreds of informal
interactions take place every day among members that communicate, test, clarify, and affirm the nature of this culture.

Coaching is fundamentally an infinitely large set of informal
and formal interactions which take place when one person who
is trying to help another person. We seriously limit our understanding of coaching and its potential, however, if we think
of it as only a transaction between individuals. Coaching is
emerging as a required function of both team leaders and
leaders of whole organizations.

In 1991 I published *Developing Superior Work Teams*. The
study described in that book involved some 25 organizations,
200 teams, and interviews with over 2000 team members. One
finding of the study was that superior teams are characterized
by having leaders who function as coaches and who are valued
for this. Since publishing my own study, the emerging team
leadership function of coaching has been verified and docu-
mented by many others. For example, a review of the development and use of teams in 20 organizations, published in 1994,
underscored the importance and need for leaders to coach new
teams and associated the success of teams with their being

coached (Wellins, Byham and Dixon, 1994). One of the organizations included in the study was Eastman Chemical Company, Tennessee Eastman Division. When the company began to move towards being a team-centred organization, it redefined supervisors as team leaders and identified coaching as one of their primary functions. In 1993 Eastman Chemical won the Malcolm Baldrige National Quality Award (the most prestigious award for quality in the United States). The authors of the study concluded that:

> Coaching effectiveness is critical in the transition to an empowered, self-directed team environment, making the development of coaches one of the keys to the process.

It is, of course, not only traditional, functionally aligned work groups which are making the transition into new ways of operating. Teams are microcosms of what is going on in whole organizations.

Change is not a periodic event in organizations. It is continuous and rapid. The demand to find increasingly better ways to manufacture, to find quicker ways to bring new products to the marketplace, to reduce service turnaround time are facts of life. Impermanence is more than a philosophical or religious idea. The truth of Heraclitus' dictum that 'change alone is unchanging' is something every person in every organization experiences at first hand.

Restructuring, realigning, downsizing, the continuous improvement of work systems, the ever-increasing pressure to do more for less are only the more obvious examples of change. In the midst of change and the drive for improved performance, CEOs and managers of large organizational units are recognizing the importance of their own coaching functions. The best of them know they must spend time communicating and clarifying goals, helping people build concrete pictures of their futures in the organization, responding to questions about uncertainties and listening to the suggestions and concerns of the people who do the work (Tichy and Charan, 1995).

KEY IDEAS

This book communicates several ideas, which are worth summarizing at the outset and are repeated frequently throughout.

1. Coaching can play a significant role in organizational performance. Understood as a personal interaction, either formal or informal, between a person who assumes the function of coach and any set of other people, coaching is a performance improvement function which has unlimited application and utility. Coaching is a real-time response to issues, needs and opportunities as they develop.

2. Anyone can be a coach and everyone should be a coach. Coaching has little to do with one's status or position in an organization. Certainly, it is a leadership activity, but it is a leadership activity that can be performed by anyone who wants to help others. It is not a function of rank or position. It is a function of desire, opportunity, and discipline.

3. Being a coach, does not always necessitate knowing more than the people being coached. In fact, the coach may often know a good deal less about any particular subject than the person being coached. Helping others solve problems does not require knowing the solution. What is required is that the coach knows how to conduct a conversation so that relevant information is developed, all alternatives are considered and decisions are made collaboratively.

4. Coaching does more than achieve the obvious results of improved performance. It connects people with people. It builds trust and positive relationships. We all respond with deepened respect to people who have helped us to learn and solve problems. When we coach others, we are compelled to look beyond the limits of our own jobs. We are made to take an active role in the development of others. Coaching helps build community within organizations. It helps reduce strident competitiveness and forces people to see their own success as being linked to that of all their co-workers.

THE PURPOSES OF THIS BOOK

The general purpose of this book is to give managers and human resource development professionals a complete understanding of the meaning and potential use of coaching which they can use to improve the performance of individuals, teams, and (ultimately) whole organizations. The specific purposes of the book are to:

1.   demonstrate the importance and power of coaching as a performance management and improvement function;
2.   develop a comprehensive definition of coaching which takes into account the many ways that coaching is currently understood and applied;
3.   provide a model that can be used to guide one's development as a coach;
4.   identify the generic skills that winning coaches use;
5.   show how to coach individuals;
6.   show how to coach teams; and
7.   show individuals how to improve their coaching skills.

OVERVIEW

CHAPTER 1   THE VALUE OF COACHING

Coaching has a remarkable track record for endurance and relevance. To begin to build a comprehensive model of coaching, we need to understand why coaching has been such a formidable and valuable means for improving the performance of individuals, teams, and organizations. This chapter provides a rationale for spending time understanding coaching and equipping ourselves to be better coaches.

CHAPTER 2   THE NATURE OF COACHING

We cannot make the most use of coaching until we define as concretely as possible just what we mean by it – that is, what coaching is and what it is not. This chapter examines the various ways in which coaching has been understood, looks at how the term is applied to what people actually do as coaches, and builds a synthesis which takes into account how coaching is applied in the world of work and organizations. The definition provides the grounding for the Successful Coaching Model which is developed in Chapter 3.

CHAPTER 3   THE SUCCESSFUL COACHING MODEL

Nothing is more useful than having a mental image of what we are trying to do – be it build a house, write a book or improve a work process. This chapter gives a picture of what coaching is. It describes the key elements in coaching interactions, the instrumental results that can be achieved in these interactions and the winning outcomes that we can expect from successful coaching.

CHAPTER 4   THE COACHING INTERACTION

The key to successful coaching is the coaching interaction. It is this element which can be most directly managed and influenced by the coach. Instrumental results flow from successful interactions and winning outcomes flow from instrumental results. This chapter provides a full treatment of the four sub-elements in the coaching interaction: beliefs, qualities, skills and process.

CHAPTER 5   COACHING IN ACTION

The general application of coaching is the continuous improvement of performance. There are, however, a number of subsets to this. Sometimes, coaching means giving feedback or encourage-ment, or supporting another person's performance. At other times, it means teaching, or solving problems or adjusting perfor-mance. This chapter describes the various ways that coaching is applied for the continuous improvement of performance, along with special skills that are relevant to each of these applications.

CHAPTER 6   COACHING WINNING TEAMS

Coaching teams is increasingly becoming a function of team leaders and team leadership. Although coaching teams shares much in common with coaching individuals, coaches need some special skills related to team meetings and team dynam-ics. This chapter describes these special skills.

CHAPTER 7   BECOMING A SUCCESSFUL COACH

This book is intended as a practical tool for anyone who wants to become a better coach. Whereas the earlier chapters provide the background and understanding required to become a better coach, this chapter defines the specific strategies and actions that anyone can use to increase their ability to coach others.

CHAPTER

7

THE VALUE OF COACHING

This book proposes that coaching is a critical strategy for the continuous improvement of the performance of individuals, teams, and, ultimately, total organizations. However, to justify the kind of investment required to become a consistently successful coach requires a strong rationale.

Why we should endorse coaching as a major organizational performance strategy and why each of us should spend time developing ourselves as coaches are questions that can be answered from two perspectives: first, coaching works; second, coaching has special relevance to the needs of modern organizations.

 ## COACHING WORKS

My rationale for coaching, my rationale for writing this book and my rationale for challenging my readers to become better coaches are based, first of all, on the demonstrable fact that coaching works. It has a proven track record. Coaching improves the performance of individuals, of teams, and of organizations. But the persistence of coaching cannot be accounted for just because it changes performance. In certain organizations, significant improvements in performance are unlikely to occur, regardless of the kind and level of effort that individuals might expend. Governmental organizations are, for example, often so inured to the need for change, that improved performance on any significant scale is highly unlikely. But even in organizational environments where little change is made in total performance, coaching continues to survive.

We can obtain a good understanding of why coaching works by analysing further these characteristics:

1.   Coaching seems to be fad-proof. It finds its own relevant place, whatever else may change in organizations. It persists and continues to be valued as an important strategy for improving performance, despite transitory 'flavour-of-the-month' organizational development and performance improvement strategies.

2.   Coaching is not dependent on the organizational environment in which it occurs.

3.   Coaching has a special potency for improving performance because of its interpersonal dimension.

4.   Coaching works because it is a self-reinforcing process.

COACHING IS FAD-PROOF

Over many years coaching has been proven to be a remarkably persistent and widely used means for improving performance. It seems to be fad-proof. The literature that has been created around the subject has been published at a steady rate for at least 20 years. Testimonies to the benefits of coaching will typically be found in at least some business and training publications almost every month. Merely reviewing the articles, books and training packages on coaching published in the last two years would be a formidable task.

Fads may come and fads may go, but coaching seems to continue forever. In fact, each time some new concept or some new way to 'fix' organizations is proposed, coaching finds a new niche or is elevated to a new level of prominence.

The several popular ways to improve organizations often involve little more than organizing people into new teams or developing existing work groups into teams – for example, re-engineering, process management, Total Quality Management and empowering. Each one of these initiatives finally requires someone to coach these teams into winning performance units.

Teams do not become superior unless they have available leaders who are coaches (Kinlaw, 1991). Nor can they manage the many different performance variables that they must manage unless there is someone available who can give the team feedback, guide, teach, challenge and support team members – in other words, *coach*.

Coaching works at every level. It works to improve the performance of individuals (including the top executives of companies), it works to improve the performance of teams and, ultimately, it works to improve the performance of entire organizations. Consider a few examples of the power of coaching in action.

Ameritech Corporation has US$23 billion in assets and about 70 000 employees. Its CEO, Bill Weiss, has ensured the company's continued success by instituting rigorous training, coaching and evaluation systems. The change brought about by Weiss institutionalized feedback and coaching throughout the executive and management levels of the company (Rao, 1994).

At Vanity Fair Mills, Jackson, Alabama, USA, a new product line was introduced. The introduction of the new product was fraught with problems, from design to production. The plant manager was able to avoid a costly disaster by modifying his own behaviour and concentrating on coaching people to fully use their experience and skills to solve the problems (Christmas, 1994).

In 1993 a metropolitan hospital in New England employed a coach for a top executive and a manager who were supposed to work closely together, but who were not performing very well. The Human Resources Director of the hospital reports that, as a result, the executive and the manager made a complete turnaround and became a high performing team (Anonymous, 1994).

Quite apart from what I read and what I know is being proposed by suppliers of training and consulting services, my own personal experience validates the importance of coaching and the value placed on it. Over the past 30 years I have owned three companies that have offered services for manager and employee training and organizational development. I have also written some 12 books about human and organizational performance. From a consultant's perspective, I can affirm that coaching skills is the training topic which has always been in demand and has always been needed to support whatever other kinds of training my companies have offered. Leaders require coaching skills to manage change. Team leaders require coaching skills to support the development and performance of their teams. Sales managers require coaching skills to train their sales people. On-the-job training, whatever the topic, requires people who have coaching skills. Customer service is improved by coaching people how to respond to the expectations and irritations of their customers.

Every performance function of every organization has benefited from coaching for as long as people have shared information about performance and how to improve it. Every performance function of every organization continues to benefit from coaching regardless of 'paradigm shift', 'culture change', 'transformation', 'downsizing' or 'pyramid inversion'. Coaching reaches something so fundamental, so practical and so congruent with improving performance that it just 'goes with the territory'.

The past and present of coaching predict its future. It is impossible to imagine a time when workers cannot be helped by more experienced workers. It is impossible to imagine a time when managers and other leaders will not need to develop people's competency and confidence to get the most from them. Coaching is too closely tied to the improvement of performance to ever become out-of-date. It is as current as any special popular plan or proposal for improving the performance of organizations, teams and individuals – whatever that plan or proposal might be.

COACHING WORKS WHATEVER THE ORGANIZATIONAL ENVIRONMENT

A second attribute of coaching that seems to explain its longevity as a performance-enhancer is its ability to make at least some positive contribution to performance, regardless of the supportive quality of the organization's environment.

Organizations and their environments are confused when leaders are ambivalent about the organization's fundamental purposes or core values. Conflicting signals are communicated and environments contaminated when people are trained to work in ways which are not consonant with the performance expectations stipulated by their superiors – this often happens when team development is introduced without first providing the necessary systems support. At times, people can be so confused about priorities and how they are expected to perform that they exist in states bordering on what sociologists call *anomie* – that is, states of lawlessness. Nevertheless, regardless of what exists in an organizational environment and despite the poor quality of an organization's environment, people are still helped by coaching and good coaches are highly valued. In short, coaching contributes something positive, in spite of negative work conditions.

I am not arguing that coaching has no relationship to organizational environments nor denying there are factors in organizational environments which are preconditions for making the *best* use of coaching. I am maintaining that one proven aspect of coaching – the one that has given it such value – is that it is something that we can give and receive, which is always useful regardless of the quality of the environment in which it takes place and no matter how incongruent that environment is with coaching.

Certainly, coaching can be a greater functional asset in organizational environments in which the organization's goals and priorities are clear – that is, where everyone knows how to score points against the competition and how to win the game. Coaching can more easily become integrated into the performance of leaders when it is easy for people to question and speak out. It has more potential in organizations which hold their leaders responsible as coaches and train them accordingly. Coaching certainly takes root and flourishes best in organizations that place a high priority on continuous learning.

Of course, coaching can never be unrelated to the organizational environment but its great strength resides in this. Coaching can produce improvement in performance, *regardless of the degree of support provided by an organization's environment.*

Some years ago, I delivered coaching training for middle managers in a large engineering corporation. At the time, the company was in a state of considerable confusion about its goals: it had no explicit strategic plan. Changes were taking place in most of its senior leadership positions; the CEO had resigned, and the company was being directed by an interim appointee. My coaching skills training session was part of a larger, two-week manager development programme. My lasting memories from this experience are:

1. The managers participating in the programme took every opportunity to voice their sense of confusion and lack of direction.
2. They complained about their own lack of influence and feelings of powerlessness.
3. They nevertheless had no difficulty accepting that learning how to become better coaches would benefit them and their organization.

In my view, these managers perceived coaching as one function that they could at least perform with purpose and some success, despite the current condition of their organization. It gave them an alternative to complaining and feeling powerless. It focused them on something that they could do – and do better – without anyone's permission. In fact, they saw coaching as a means of helping their co-workers cope with the organization's unstable condition.

Another example which illustrates why coaching, as an individually initiated action, has such value, occurred when a colleague of mine was delivering a large-scale team development programme for a service organization. The CEO had decreed that there would be team development, without gaining any commitment from senior managers, middle managers or supervisors. My colleague recognized, of course, that one task that team leaders would have to undertake was to help their teams develop their own strategies for developing and performing as teams even if their own managers were passive, or even aggressively negative, about the process. By training the team leaders as team coaches, she was able to achieve some good results from team training, despite the organizational environment in which the training was delivered.

In summary the second attribute of coaching that accounts for its continued persistence and success is that it works even in environments which are confused and which provide it with little or no support.

THE PERSONAL NATURE OF COACHING

The third attribute of coaching that seems to explain its persistence and argue for its continued uses as a major performance improvement strategy is its personal nature. Because coaching takes place between a person functioning as a coach and one or more other persons who are being coached, it is a personal transaction and always has a personal dimension. While it is true that executives cannot coach their organizations until they have identified the few important improvement goals or objectives of the organization, it is also through the many interpersonal conversations held between executives and their managers and employees that these priorities are clarified and made vitally relevant to the performance of each manager and employee.

None of the above is to deny the importance of formal training. The rapid changes in technology demand continuous update and training. No organization will ever acquire and keep customers for life, unless every person in the organization has the knowledge and skill required to assess customer satisfaction, to consult with customers and translate customer discontent into specific improvements. To build this kind of knowledge and skill in people requires a good deal of formal training. However they are organized, teams can never develop into superior teams without it. But it is often the personal conversations that people trained for some competency hold with those people who already have that competency that make training take 'root'. Even within the limits of a training programme, it is often the instructor coaching students and students coaching other students that makes the training work.

'People need people', to learn and to improve their performance. People need to be challenged by others to think more clearly and to perform better. There seems to be no substitute for the interpersonal dimension in performance. Coaching – understood as the multitude of performance-related conversations which we have with each other – exists by means of its own necessity and continues through its own appropriateness. It responds to our personal need to reduce uncertainty.

The fundamental characteristic of every organization is that it processes information: it uses information, it creates information and it outputs information. But transmitted information is always full of *noise*. It is full of ambiguities, gaps and errors. Coaching, understood as a conversation between people, is one of the means that organizations have for managing these ambiguities, gaps and errors. Coaching tutors, clarifies and confirms. Coaching corrects and completes what is intended in directives, manuals and every other form of written communication. It reduces people's uncertainties about their performance through feedback and reduces uncertainty in many other ways.

The interpersonal nature of coaching largely accounts for its recognized value. In coaching conversations we can learn what we know we need to learn by simply asking questions about it. Learning is no longer generalized, it is personalized. A true coaching conversation is mutual, balanced and two-way. It gives clarity about performance goals and expectations; it helps us resolve our own personal performance problems; it reveals our blind spots; it gives us the encouragement and confidence to accept more difficult challenges.

The continuing value of coaching and its persistence as a performance management and improvement strategy often comes down finally to nothing more complicated than the fact that human conversation is the means by which performance is often best managed and improved.

COACHING IS SELF-REINFORCING

When I use the term *coaching*, I mean, of course, *successful coaching* – in other words coaching that accomplishes the ultimate goal of achieving winning outcomes or of attaining one or more instrumental goals such as creating clarity, increasing competency or strengthening confidence. All of the results that coaching produces cannot be immediately demonstrated at the end of a coaching conversation. But some results are *always* evident at that point. It is because coaching always results in one or more of these immediate satisfactory outcomes that it is self-reinforcing for both the person coaching and the people being coached.

It is common knowledge that we are motivated to continue any activity or behaviour which results in an outcome that we value – that is, a personally rewarding result. Some years ago I developed and verified an Integrated Model of Motivation (Kinlaw, 1991). This model identified the three most important variables accounting for the strength of people's motivation to do their jobs the very best that they can all of the time. They are *Match, Return,* and *Expectation.*

Match refers to the decision that we make about the degree to which something we are doing, something we plan to do or some goal that we want to achieve is congruent with what we value. It principally describes the many *intrinsic* rewards that we obtain or expect.

Return describes the kind and amount of *extrinsic* reward that we get from taking some action, the amount of reward that we expect to get from taking some action or the amount of reward we expect to get by achieving some goal. We feel extrinsically rewarded when we feel that our time has been well spent and when we feel that our efforts have been appropriately acknowledged by others through the various rewards and accolades that we value.

Expectation is the third factor in the motivation equation. It is the degree of confidence that we have in performing some task at hand, or the confidence we feel that we will be able to perform some task in the future, or the confidence that we feel in attaining some future goal. Expectation is influenced by the competencies we have, the resources we have and the number and severity of the obstacles to our performance that we anticipate.

Match, Return, and Expectation are all relevant to coaching success and help explain its persistence and popularity. However, Match demonstrates further why coaching is a self-reinforcing activity.

We are continually making a judgement about the degree of match, or congruence, between what we value and what we do or want to achieve – that is, our goals. The closer the match between what we value and what we do or want to achieve, the stronger is our motivation to act. Match is a measurement of anticipated or actual *intrinsic* reward – in other words, the value of doing the activity itself. Sailors, like myself, like to sail for the sailing itself, regardless of where we are going and regardless of whether we win a race. Gardening often provides the same sort of match between what we do and the rewards we get for doing it. Even if our daffodils have stalks that are too short or never flower at all, we will plant them again for the pure pleasure of planting.

Coaching provides intrinsic rewards to both the person coaching and the person being coached. I know from my own experience what some of these are, but I suspect there are a number of others which I have not identified. Some of the intrinsic rewards that coaches gain are as follows:

1. Coaching provides an intrinsic reward because it is something that we can do on our own initiative. We don't need anyone's permission to coach, except that of the people being coached. The freedom to act is, in itself, reinforcing because most of us value such freedom and see ourselves as the kind of people who will act independently to improve ourselves and others.

2. Coaching provides an intrinsic reward because we feel valued in the process of coaching. When others gain clarity, learning and insight from our coaching, when they resolve problems and gain greater confidence through our coaching, they value us and we are rewarded by being valued.

3. Coaching often leads to new learning for the coach, and learning is a self-rewarding activity. Because successful coaching is always a mutual, interactive, two-way process of communication, the coach will typically learn something useful in every coaching conversation.

Coaching also provides a solid match for persons being coached between what they value and the process of coaching. Here are some of the ways that coaching is intrinsically rewarding for people being coached.

1. Good coaches listen. Just being listened to by another person is a rewarding experience, even if all our problems are not resolved and all our questions are not answered.

2. Successful coaching conversations are always concrete and people being coached are helped to become more and more specific about what they need to know or the problems they need to resolve. Knowing is more satisfying than not knowing. Certainty is more satisfying than

uncertainty. We like to be coached because we like knowing and we like certainty.

3. When we are in conversation with good coaches, we feel rewarded *within* the conversation, regardless of what we achieve *by* the conversation. During successful coaching conversations we feel respected because our questions, our ideas and our contributions are always taken seriously.

SUMMARY

Coaching holds exceptional promise for managing and improving performance and, because of this, merits our attention and our commitment. The first element in my rationale to justify learning how to coach and becoming a better coach is simply that it works. It works because:

1. It is fad-proof. It persists and it continues to be valued as a major strategy for improving performance, whatever the current fashion in organizational development happens to be.
2. It is not dependent on the organizational environment in which it occurs.
3. It has special potency for improving performance because of its interpersonal dimension.
4. It is a self-reinforcing process.

 # THE RELEVANCE OF COACHING

The second element in my rationale for coaching is that it has a special relevancy to the conditions and needs of modern organizations. It has always been useful, if not critical, for people who know how to perform some task to show others, who are not as skilled, how to perform that task and improve the way they do it. It has always been a function of leadership to motivate, to inspire and to challenge others to attempt ever higher levels of performance.

Resolving the performance problems of co-workers has always been a responsibility of leaders such as managers and supervisors. Giving concrete and performance-related feedback to people has always been a predictably useful means for moulding their skills and performance. Keeping individuals and teams focused on achieving specific performance goals has been an invariable characteristic of the best leadership.

As I have demonstrated above, coaching, in its many shapes and functions, is hardly a new supervisory or leadership function. It is probably as old as organizations themselves. But, nowadays, there is a new coaching imperative: unless organizations make coaching a corporate strategy they will not be able to manage the broader spans of control created by downsizing and restructuring; they will be unable to manage the frequency and magnitude of the changes they must undertake; they will not be able to manage successfully the growth and development of teams and teamwork; and they most certainly will not make the very best use of their human resources by empowering people with new competencies and making sure that they fully use these competencies (Kinlaw, 1996a).

The position taken in this book is that coaching is a strategy whose time has fully come. Organizations which will achieve and maintain records of superior performance will be those which have fully exploited the strategy of coaching. This proposition can be supported in a number of ways.

First, organizations will undoubtedly remain under tremendous pressure to do more with less, in order to stay competitive. Downsizing, running lean and mean and radically reducing overheads are conditions under which all organizations must now function (Hankins and Kleiner, 1995; Kinlaw, 1996a). Our traditional expectations of company managers and other leaders no longer meet the needs of modern organizations, any more than traditional systems or structures do. Modern organizations are becoming flat and seamless structures in which traditional management hierarchies, control pyramids, job descriptions, direct supervision and the strict separation between labour and management are becoming less and less useful. They are finding ways to do more with ever-decreasing overheads and are rapidly changing to team-centred structures of empowered employees. These modern, team centred, empowered organizations need modern leaders.

In modern organizations the span of control has often become so large that the whole concept of control must be abandoned, or at least redefined. Control can no longer mean direct supervision. The possibility of overseeing – that is, observing and controlling as the root meaning of supervision suggests – is increasingly impossible. It is not even clear whether the traditional tools of overseeing, such as performance appraisals, can work under conditions of less and less direct supervision. How can supervisors appraise not only what people do, but *how* they do it, when they may be the reporting senior for a hundred or more people? 'Supervisor', 'supervise' and 'supervision' are on their way to becoming terms that can have a precise meaning only in institutions where inmates, not employees, are overseen and controlled.

Leading and managing by coaching is an alternative to leading and managing by direct control. It is an alternative which is fully congruent with the realities that govern the shape and performance of modern organizations. When leaders and managers concentrate on continually improving performance and maximizing the intellectual resources which are available to make such an improvement, they will make more and more use of management and leadership strategies which focus on setting values, setting goals and giving rewards. They will devote increasingly less attention on directing day-to-day operations, limiting what people can and cannot do and checking up on what people have done or not done. They will approach the issue of control from the perspective of how to release the intellectual energy of every member of their organizations to improve performance (Kinlaw, 1996a).

Coaching is a proven way of releasing people's mental energy. It is directed towards guiding people toward the organization's goals by building commitment to these goals and the competence to reach them. Coaching is one very important way to ensure sustained superior performance and the continuous improvement of performance *when performance can no longer be continually and directly observed.* Coaching, to be sure, requires observation. But it is *selective* observation. It is observation used as a basis for learning, challenging and improving. It is not observation for controlling.

A second reason why coaching has special relevance today in leading, managing and working is that the rules for competing, surviving and growing – that is, *the rules for winning* – have changed from what they were even ten years ago, and we can expect these rules to keep changing and the difference between what was and what is to become increasingly pronounced. More importantly, we can expect rapid and unexpected change to become a given condition of organizational life. The challenge facing organizations is whether they can meet the demand to develop people who can lead, work and win under the new rules.

Change is no longer the slow process which could be understood as moving from a stable state, passing through an unstable state and moving on to a new stable state. Stable states are becoming ever more elusive. Working in highly unstable states will become the increasingly pervasive condition for work, workers and organizations.

The traditional roles and functions of managers and other leaders developed in times when people still believed that organizations were successful because managers were able to get employees to do what they were directed to do. The reality in modern organizations is that employees must initiate more and more actions without waiting for approval, and leaders must spend more and more time being resources, managing processes, stimulating innovation and keeping everyone focused on the organization's goals in the midst of changes, changes to changes and changes to changes to changes.

Coaching, as a strategy for managing and improving performance, has a particular (if not unique) relevance to change. We cannot predict for most workers, for any given period, exactly what must be done, what special initiatives they should take, or what problems will emerge as priorities which must be immediately resolved. Under conditions of continuous and rapid change, managers and supervisors serve their organization's performance goals best when they act as information links and keep people up-to-date on what is happening and what is probably going to happen – in other words, when they *coach* people how to prepare for the expected and how to manage the unexpected. They manage performance in the midst of change by keeping people focused on achieving customer satisfaction, regardless of turbulence in the organization. They serve as resources and problem solvers. In short, they coach.

A third reason for claiming that coaching has special relevancy to the needs of today's organizations is that the customer (both internal and external) has now been crowned monarch to preside over the destinies of organizations. They have the power of life and death. Their decisions cannot be overruled. We live in the age of the customer. Customers are increasingly becoming the most powerful arbiters of quality. *External* customers have, of course, always had the power of the purse. They could buy or not buy. They could choose among alternative sources for their services and products. But now it is not only external customers who are demanding satisfaction. Enter the *internal* customer.

Individuals and teams who receive any input within a work process are the customers of the individuals or teams providing that input. It has become apparent that organizations cannot satisfy their external customers unless they satisfy their internal customers. Unless every single work process delivers to its *internal* customers products and services which are 100 per cent fit to use 100 per cent of the time, the organization cannot possibly deliver products and services to its *external* customers which satisfy the same criteria.

Coaching is especially relevant to gaining and maintaining the satisfaction of internal and external customers. Co-workers can coach their colleagues in real time by observing the way they respond to customers, by giving feedback and by suggesting improvements. Sales managers can accompany their sales personnel when they make calls and carry out 'kerbstone' coaching immediately following a call. More experienced people can model desired performance to less experienced people for any function that bears on customer satisfaction.

Customers expect immediate attention to be given to their problems. They expect immediate improvement in the way their concerns and their accounts are managed. Coaching is a particularly powerful means for creating immediate improvement and therefore a most effective way to improve customer satisfaction.

Managing customer satisfaction requires direct and frequent contact. It requires that immediate response be given to customer concerns and complaints. The people most qualified to respond to the needs of customers are the people who are most directly involved in serving their needs – that is, those who deliver the services and products. Successful customer service is a function of how well coached the people are who serve the customer.

There is another, and easily overlooked, shape that coaching can take in managing customer satisfaction. How often do we hear suppliers, in describing their internal or their external customers, complain because these customers 'have unrealistic expectations', 'don't understand the problem', 'can't stand to be told "no"', and the like. Of course, it is true that we can become the victims of inappropriate and unrealistic expectations from our customers and that customers can sometimes make demands that no one can fulfil. But so what? We don't get to choose our customers, we only get to serve them. One way that we can serve them is to coach them to become better customers, help them have clear expectations, help them clarify their problems and find the best answers, and help them make the best possible use of our competencies as well as our services and products.

A fourth reason that coaching is particularly appropriate as an important strategy for the continuous improvement of performance in today's organizations is that the proven key to improvement and sustained superior performance is competent people. Systems don't change and improve organizations, people do. None of the organizational development fads such as re-engineering or Total Quality Management will change organizations and improve performance unless competent people become more competent and the most competent people have the most influence most of the time (Kinlaw, 1996a).

No company can afford the luxury of not fully developing the competencies of its people. No company can run the risk of making the wrong decisions, solving the wrong problems and wasting time and money by not fully using the competencies of its workforce.

Not all leaders have fully understood that they really have two jobs: first, developing competent people and, second, removing the organizational barriers that inhibit the full use of competent people. There are still too many people trying to *put new wine into old wineskins*. Some people have not yet realized that the old inefficient ways of doing business are gone forever. Doing more with less means attending to quality. Coaching develops commitment to excellence. It develops competence and it develops confidence. People who are well coached will attempt more and contribute more than those who are not well coached. Coaching makes sure that people climb the positive slope of continuous improvement and that they know how to contribute to the organization's continuous improvement.

Coaching, when rightly understood and correctly applied, is a strategy unequalled in its capacity to ensure that the right people with the right competencies perform the right tasks in the right way. It is a strategy for developing individuals and teams, as well as whole organizations. It is the right strategy for moving whole organizations towards superior performance and continuous improvement. It is also the right strategy for gaining the commitment of teams and individuals to support the organization's performance goals by doing their very best all of the time.

 ## SUMMARY

The answer to the question, 'Why should we invest time and effort in understanding coaching and developing ourselves as better coaches?' has two parts. First, coaching has a proven track record. It works and it has demonstrated its worth in managing and improving performance for as long as people have been placed together in organizations. Second, coaching has special relevance to the needs of today's organizations.

The following chapters provide an understanding of coaching and describe the qualities and skills of successful coaching as a guide to developing superior ability. The first step in this process is to build a specific definition of coaching which can be used as a starting point in our journey towards being superior coaches.

CHAPTER

2

THE NATURE OF COACHING

The first step in developing ourselves as successful coaches (and in helping others become successful coaches) is to have a definition of coaching which can guide this development. What is needed is no theoretical definition. We need a definition which captures the full reality of coaching as coaching is understood and actually practised. Coaching, as a term, cannot mean everything or anything if it is to have any practical use. Nevertheless, when we define the term, we must try and include everything that our experience and wisdom know to be coaching activities.

The definition which I will develop in this chapter is based on some 30 years of observing coaches in action, of questioning people about their best coaches, of publishing books and training materials on coaching, and of delivering coaching skills workshops for several thousands of people.

 ## COACHING IS NOT A ROLE, IT IS A FUNCTION

Before describing what coaching is, I need to emphasize what coaching is not. It is not a role. It is a function. It is a leadership function that anyone can use and one that everyone *should* use. However, whatever else I am advocating in this book, I am not advocating that we eliminate all the traditional management functions of leaders and reduce all leadership functions to the single function of coaching.

Turning leaders into coaches does not necessarily lead to the greater involvement of people and greater empowerment. Coaches can be just as despotic as traditional leaders. Most of our images of coaches are derived from the world of athletics – and I know of no more controlling person than an athletic coach!

Making coaching a strategy for producing winning individuals and winning teams does not mean keeping the power to direct and control in the hands of leaders and merely changing the titles 'supervisor' and 'manager' to 'coach'. Leaders have many other tasks to carry out. They must give strategic direction, plan, organize, staff and allocate resources. They must make decisions about organizational changes and integrate the many separate organizational units into a fully aligned entity. Yet they have to learn to do all of these things by involving the workforce in increasingly creative ways. They must also learn how to make full use of all their human resources and build team-centred organizations. In addition to all these activities and tasks, they must also coach, and they will spend more time coaching than carrying out more traditional functions. This change is particularly obvious in companies that have shifted to a team-centred organization. One US firm, Bechton, Dickinson and Company, maintains that, whereas coaching and training took 10 per cent of a supervisor's time prior to the move to teams, coaching and training now take 60 per cent of a supervisor's time (Wellins, Byham, and Wilson, 1991).

 ## COACHING: A WINNING DEFINITION

As I begin to build a definition of coaching, I am conscious of one primary desire. I want to build a definition that will drive action. I want to describe coaching in such a concrete way that no one will have any doubt about its exact goals, its exact functions, its applications, and the competencies needed to practise it. I want to demonstrate clearly the connection between coaching and the creation of winning individuals, winning teams and winning organizations. In order to do this, we must first acknowledge the many different ways that coaching is used. In this way, we can begin to build a definition that both takes into account these many uses and includes all that is common to them.

THE MANY FACES OF COACHING

Coaching is commonly associated with games and competition. The coaches who spring most quickly to mind are probably those who coach football, baseball, basketball, tennis, cricket, track and the many other kinds of competitive athletic teams. Coaches may also be found in non-athletic areas. People who play competitive chess have coaches. Those who play competitive bridge and those who participate in team debates have coaches. Even those who participate in beauty competitions have coaches.

Coaching is also a familiar function in the arts. Dramatic coaches and voice coaches abound. Like all coaches, the ones who coach players and divas do more than just teach. They guide individuals towards a better understanding of, and fulfilling, their own goals and potential.

Coaching in athletics and the arts is reasonably well defined. We can be reasonably confident that, when we talk about coaching a team or a singer, we will be understood. What comes to mind is one person teaching others, helping others fine-tune their skills, providing guidance, challenging others and encouraging others. Coaching people to sing, write or play also means helping people find their blind spots. It means giving people information which they could not obtain for themselves about their performance. When we talk about coaching in organizations, we cannot be so certain that we will be understood.

Although coaching has been viewed as a management function and the term has been in general use in organizations from at least the early part of the twentieth century, it is still not a well defined term and we cannot presume to know immediately what is meant by it. As recently as six or eight years ago, coaching was typically combined with the term 'coun-selling' or taken to be synonymous with it (Kinlaw, 1989). Although, this association seems to be becoming less common-place today, the meaning of coaching, as the term is used in organizations, is still very imprecise.

Some of this confusion over definition arises because coach-ing is so widely and diversely applied. Giving feedback is sometimes equated with coaching (Robertson-Saunders, 1991; Aurelio and Kennedy, 1991). Coaching is applied to the concept of self-managed career counselling (Koonce, 1995). Coaching is used to describe the image that chief executive officers want to create of themselves (Tichy and Charan, 1995; Brewer, 1995; Kiechel, 1991). Coaching is equated with on-the-job training. It is identified as a way to help people create their ideal life style (Chari, 1995).

None of these definitions or descriptions of the functions of coaching is wrong. Certainly, some are fairly arbitrary and some are unnecessarily vague. The difficulty with them is that they all adopt a single, very circumscribed, approach to coaching. What are the characteristics that they all share in common? Where are the unifying principles? These are the questions that I will answer in this book, beginning with my definition of coaching.

Another source of confusion about coaching in organiza-tions is attempts are often made to use models from athletic coaching and apply these naively to the very different worlds of private and public organizations. Athletics coaches have been interviewed and the insights that these coaches have about building successful athletic teams are applied to coach-ing people at work (see Mcnutt, 1995; Knippen and Green, 1990). Athletics coaches are even called in by organizations to teach managers how to coach (Luke and Berney, 1995).

THE MODEL FROM ATHLETICS

There are, of course, a number of common attributes that coach-ing and its purposes share in athletics and in business organi-zations. For example, coaching in both settings is devoted to winning, be it a game, survival or higher profits. But coaching has a different shape in these two settings because organizations and work differ from athletic teams in a number of very significant ways.

As I have suggested above, using an athletic model for coaching is to use a mistaken analogy because coaches in athletics possess and use power in a way that may lead to superior performance on the playing field but which does not lead to superior performance in the world of work. The athletics model of a coach is not very far removed from the traditional role that some leaders of organizations have adopted in the past – that of benevolent dictator. These types of coach decide who will play and how play will be conducted, and they exercise immediate and direct supervision of what players are doing and not doing.

Athletics teams have a limited number of problems to solve whereas organizations have an unlimited number of problems to solve. Games last a given period and players need only do their best for this defined period but the work of organizations continues unceasingly, until the organization disappears. Consequently people in organizations must be doing their best all of the time indefinitely.

The complexity of the kind of competition and the requirements for continuous improvement are much higher in organizations than in athletics. An organization may be competing with a number of other organizations simultaneously; teams play one team at a time. Organizations simply require a lot more creative thought and behaviour than teams ever do. Coaching in organizations will usually be much more complex than coaching an athletics team.

Athletics teams usually have the luxury of trading, buying, and selling new players to improve their performance. Organizations must often improve the performance of the people they have and are constrained by a variety of laws and labour agreements in hiring and firing.

Finally, athletic games have much to do with mental and physical coordination. One professional player of American football once told me, 'good coaches make you want to go out there and really hurt somebody and keep hurting somebody'. This kind of motivation may work in team sports, but where is its place in an organization that is carrying out research or performing some other highly cognitive activity? Organizations rarely need people to run faster or hit harder; they need people who think deeply and wisely. Playing a game to win and working to win are not the same thing and we cannot take the athletics model of coaching and apply it in some simple-minded way to organizations.

There is one additional difference between coaching athletic teams and coaching organizations. Underlying coaching in athletics is a control model of leadership. The coach plans the strategy of play, directs play, observes play in progress and corrects performance in progress. Coaching in organizations, as I have already shown, is a leadership strategy which has special value precisely because leading by controlling doesn't work in today's organizations.

One of the biggest challenges to anyone who wants to make coaching a principal strategy for continuous improvement is to determine exactly what is intended by the term 'coaching'. It is enough at this point simply to acknowledge that coaching is a potent idea which has proven utility for improving performance and one which exists in many shapes and forms in organizations. The many ways in which coaching is used and the many erroneous associations that people make between coaching and other activities, such as athletics, does not allow us to assume that there is no underlying common ground to coaching. In fact, there *is* such a common ground and it lies primarily in the notion of winning.

COMMON ELEMENT NO. 1: COACHING AND WINNING

With coaching existing in such dissimilar activities as football, chess, drama and singing, we can lose sight of one fundamental similarity in all types of coaching, regardless of where it occurs. In the midst of the many and diverse ways that coaching is applied and the confusion that may exist around its meaning, one thing about coaching is perfectly straightforward. Coaching is valued by organizations and their leaders as a proven way to create successful performance results.

At Mercantile, the CEO, T. H. Jacobsen attributes the company's remarkable comeback to coaching. At AlliedSignal, its

CEO, Lawrence Bossidy, assumed leadership in 1991. By 1995 the company had doubled its net income and the company's market value. Although Bossidy combined business units, coordinated company-wide functions such as purchasing and information systems, and made a number of other significant changes, he maintains that it has been his coaching of managers and employees that has developed the understanding and commitment that have resulted in AlliedSignal's success.

Jack Welsh, CEO of General Electric, affirms that performance at General Electric is dependent on fulfilling his role as coach. By coaching he is able to keep the best and brightest people. By coaching he is able to get people to do their best, bring our their best ideas, and keep them focused on what is of immediate importance (Bennis, 1995).

The people involved in coaching may change. The qualities of coaching may change. The skills required for a good coach may vary because they depend on whether it is individuals or teams which are being coached. But one thing about coaching stays the same. People are coached to *win* and coaching is successful when it results in *winning*. In the world of business, as well as in the worlds of the arts and athletics, coaches coach to win and people look to coaching to help them win.

Amidst great variety in definition and application, all coaching rests on the common ground of having winning as a goal. We can therefore use the idea of winning to begin building a definition of coaching.

Coaching produces winning results for individuals, teams, and organizations.

COMMON ELEMENT NO. 2: GOAL-SPECIFIC PERFORMANCE

Winning can never be pursued directly without cheating. When organizations and people pursue winning directly they will behave unethically and subvert every other value to winning. When winning at any price becomes a goal, companies sabotage their competitors' products; they steal their secrets; they lie about the health risks their products present; they falsify the data in their own research to convince the public that their products are not harmful.

When winning is made the only goal, one ice skater becomes involved in an attempt to injure a competitor, a baseball player tries to use an illegal bat, and hundreds of athletes take steroids. Pursuit of the Americas Cup leads a competitor to destroy the race's long and honoured tradition by entering a catamaran. Whatever else coaching means, it does mean coaching people to win; but it does not mean encouraging people to win at *any* price.

Coaching results in winning, but is directed at improving performance – that is, towards the continuous clarification of the goals to achieve, the increase of the knowledge and skills to achieve these goals and the removal of obstacles impeding their achievement. This focus on goals, and the alignment of performance with goals, provides us with another characteristic that unites all coaching.

There is a lesser and a greater goal dimension in successful coaching. All successful coaching directs people towards larger goals such as project completion, system improvement, cost reduction, customer satisfaction, new product generation and the like. But coaching also focuses people on the lesser or instrumental goals of gaining clarity about tasks and priorities, learning new knowledge and skills, gaining confidence to attempt more difficult tasks, exercising greater initiative and rising to higher levels of commitment to sustained superior performance. These instrumental goals can be as simple as improving presentation skills or as complex as learning to use a better strategy to reach an increased sales target, or learning better ways to improve market share, or how to apply quality management tools to achieve a new level in cost reduction.

In this book, I concentrate on coaching as a strategy for continuously improving the performance of individuals and teams. It is possible, of course, to think of coaching as something directed by executives and senior managers towards their whole organizations. Regardless of whether coaching is aimed at individuals, teams or entire organizations, it is always a goal-focused and goal-driven activity. When chief executives spend time communicating to managers, skip level groups (that is, groups that do not report directly to the executive) and the rank and file their specific improvement goals, these executives are coaching the organization. When a team leader helps a team affirm over and over again, in the midst of its many different activities, what it will achieve within some specific period of time, that leader is coaching the team. When a supervisor clarifies exactly what a co-worker is expected to accomplish, that supervisor is coaching the co-worker.

Coaches, however, do more than orient us towards specific performance improvement goals as though these could be achieved all at once and once and for all. The definition of performance goals and the refinement of these goals is a continuous process. It takes place repeatedly in multiple interactions between coaches and the people they coach.

Coaches help us clarify and reclarify our performance goals, but they also help us monitor our progress towards these goals by helping us assess our own progress and by giving us feedback on our performance.

The goals in coaching may differ in kind. They may also differ in whether they are intermediate or final goals, but coaching is very much a goal-oriented activity. This goal-oriented quality of coaching gives us another common element to build into our definition of coaching.

Coaching produces winning results for individuals, teams and organizations by focusing and refocusing them on performance goals.

COMMON ELEMENT NO. 3: COACHING IS INTERPERSONAL

In this book we are concerned with coaching as it operates at two levels – individuals and teams. Coaching may be directed towards whole organizations, but this is a limited function of executives and senior managers and requires special treatment. At whatever level coaching takes place, it is always an interpersonal interaction.

The coach can be trying to help a team better manage its team meetings. The coach may be trying to help an individual clarify a career goal, or get some task back on schedule, or learn how to use some specific tool for managing projects – such as a project scheduling or work breakdown charts. Whatever the specific performance goal that is being managed – however complex or simple – all coaching involves a conversation between the coach and some other individual or individuals.

Communicating strategic goals, communicating specific performance improvement goals and directing major changes such as moving towards self-managed teams can be attempted by impersonal communication – for example, letters, directives, memoranda, electronic mail, flyers, newsletters and posters. But this is not coaching.

All coaching is aimed at accomplishing the organization's larger performance goals. There are, however, a number of lesser goals which must be attained in order for people to achieve their performance goals. For example, they must understand the goals, they must be committed to reach the goals, and they must have the resources and the competencies to achieve the goals. Coaching achieves these lesser goals by means of conversations that are fully mutual, that have give-and-take, and which develop information required by both coach and the person coached. It is these personal interactions that build clarity, competence, confidence and commitment.

We have now identified a third element that must be included in our coaching definition. When we include the interpersonal dimension, our definition reads:

Coaching is a personal interaction with one or more persons which produces winning results for individuals, teams and organizations by focusing and refocusing them on performance goals.

COMMON ELEMENT NO. 4: DISCIPLINE

We have almost completed the working definition of coaching which will become the framework for the full development of the functions of coaching and the basis for the content of the remaining chapters in this book. We have been building this definition by searching for common ground in the many different ways that coaching is understood and applied in organizations. We have found the following common in all coaching:

one or more conversations between a coach and the persons being coached, which focuses and refocuses individuals and teams on winning performance goals.

There is another element that is necessary when we recognize that we are defining coaching as a results-oriented activity. We are interested in *successful* coaching – that is, coaching which leads to winning results. Coaching which results in winning and which focuses individuals and teams on specific performance goals is neither random nor occurs by chance. Coaching to win requires discipline. It requires discipline for coaches to discover what others know and what they don't know. It requires discipline for coaches to help people say what they need to say. It requires discipline for coaches to help people find their own solutions to their own problems. It takes discipline for coaches to confront shortfalls in performance and achieve positive results.

In the following chapters I will describe in detail just what sort of discipline coaches must have. For now it suffices to indicate that to be disciplined requires that coaches have a concrete model of coaching which guides their behaviour. They need some way to assess their own coaching behaviour and a means of identifying ways to improve their behaviour. Models can function like benchmarks. They can show us what the best practices are and help us identify improvement opportunities. One of the primary purposes of this book is to provide readers with a coaching model that they can use to clarify exactly what they need to do to coach winning individuals or teams. When we add the notion of discipline to our definition of coaching we have:

Coaching is a disciplined personal interaction with one or more persons which produces winning results for individuals, teams and organizations by focusing and refocusing them on performance goals.

ELEMENT NO. 5: COACHING AS ADDED VALUE

There is one final element needed to complete our definition of coaching. This last element clearly places the responsibility for the success of coaching on the coach. Coaching does not only focus people on performance goals, it does much, much more. Coaching provides people with what they need to achieve these goals.

Coaching helps people achieve winning performance results by facilitating their:

○   gaining greater clarity about just what their performance goals are and the specific expectations that exist around these goals

○   gaining greater clarity about how well they are doing in their efforts to attain these goals

○   overcoming blocks to achieving performance goals

○   increasing or finding out how to increase their competence for achieving these goals

○   strengthening their confidence that they can achieve the goals

○   extending and increasing the empowerment they need to initiate actions on their own to achieve the goals

○   gaining the resolve or commitment to do their utmost best 100 per cent of the time to reach the goals.

When we add the element of facilitating to our definition of coaching we have the following complete definition:

Coaching is a disciplined personal interaction with one or more persons which produces winning results for individuals, teams and organizations by focusing and refocusing them on performance goals and facilitating their achievement of these goals.

This proposed definition of coaching clearly positions coaching as an added-value function. Successful coaching is an added-value function because:

1.   It is a *personal interaction* and carries all the potential power of influence held by personal contact.

2.   It is a *disciplined personal interaction*. It is successful because of coaches' understanding of the nature of coaching, and the skills that coaches demonstrate in conducting coaching conversations. Successful coaching is not a random interchange. It always moves towards achieving some concrete goal.

3.   It is a *facilitative personal interaction* in the true meaning
     of facilitate – that is, to make easy. It directs people
     towards winning performance goals, but it also clarifies
     those goals, creates competency, develops confidence and
     increases commitment.

 ## FORMAL AND INFORMAL COACHING

Coaching is always a personal interaction. It may consist of a
very few words of feedback or encouragement. People are
coaching when they say 'Nice going. Keep up the good work'.
They are coaching when they say 'You've done a great job
mastering that new system'. They are coaching when they say
'Those changes you recommended in our scheduling process
are working out just fine'. They are coaching when they advise,
'Try the macro for that function'. They are coaching when they
say 'Remember to limit the information on those slides'.

Coaching can also be an *extended* conversation. It can
consist of helping to solve a problem which someone presents.
Coaching is taking place when one person tries to help another
develop some new skill and when, in this helping process, there
are a multitude of exchanges, questions, answers, encourage-
ments and confirmations. Coaching is taking place when a
responsible person confronts another about some problem in
performance and reaches a positive resolution.

Coaching, as a pervasive tool for the continuous improvement of performance, takes place far more often in an informal
interaction rather than a formal one. Each time a team meets,
coaching opportunities are present and can be best dealt with
in *real* time. When team members are learning to use some new
problem-solving tool, the time to coach is while they are using
the tool. When someone is working on a task and is unclear
about some aspect of it, the best time to coach is while the
person is trying to carry out that task. When a co-worker asks
for help in solving some problem, the best time to respond
is usually when the request is made. Most opportunities for

coaching occur *on the spot* – at the exact moment when some need is identified.

Informal opportunities for coaching often present themselves every time we make contact with others. When leaders practise management 'by walking around', they have unlimited opportunities to give support, encourage, express appreciation, answer questions – in other words, *coach*. When we work with our colleagues on some common task, each of us has numerous opportunities to clarify the task for each other, teach each other, build each other's confidence – in short, *coach*.

Coaching can, however, be a formal (that is, planned and structured) conversation. There are times, for example, when a leader must provide specific instruction, or address some performance problem. Such conversations should typically be conducted in private and, to be successful, usually require special preparation.

Whatever its length and whatever its degree of formality, successful coaching is always a disciplined interaction. Coaching is always focused on performance. It always has certain characteristics. It always employs a set of interpersonal skills.

As I have developed my definition of coaching, I have intended it to apply to both formal and informal coaching conversations. Coaching, however, regardless of the degree of formality or informality, always has certain qualities and requires certain skills. I describe these in detail in later chapters.

Thus far, I have developed a rationale for coaching and a definition of coaching. In the following chapter I will set out my Successful Coaching Model which will give a visual description of the elements of coaching and provide a conceptual framework for the remaining chapters in this book.

CHAPTER

3

THE SUCCESSFUL COACHING MODEL

This chapter builds up a visual description of successful coaching and suggests the remaining topics that I will cover in subsequent chapters. To understand how to become successful coaches, we must have a clear mental picture of the winning outcomes which we are trying to achieve, the instrumental results which produce these outcomes and the characteristics of successful coaching which we must create that lead to these instrumental results and final outcomes. To develop into superior coaches we need to have a plan and know exactly what knowledge and skills must be mastered.

 ## THE USES OF THE MODEL

The purpose of any descriptive model is to organize information and display that information in such a way that the relationships among various elements in some system, or among some set of variables, are clarified. The particular uses of the Successful Coaching Model (Figure 3.1) are:

○ to provide us with a graphic understanding of coaching that we can use to manage successful coaching interactions

○ to emphasize that successful coaching always means producing winning performance outcomes

○ to provide us with a framework for undertaking our own development as successful coaches

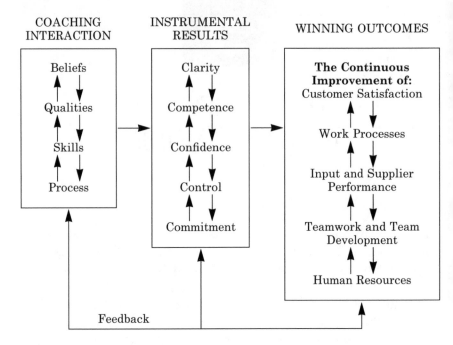

Figure 3.1 The Successful Coaching Model

○   to provide guidance for designing coaching training programmes.

 OVERVIEW OF THE MODEL

The Successful Coaching Model includes three principal elements: coaching interaction, instrumental results, and winning outcomes. The logic of the model is as follows:

1. A coach has an interaction with one or more persons.
2. If this interaction has the requisite positive characteristics it leads to certain instrumental results.
3. These instrumental results become sufficient causes for achieving and maintaining performance levels with winning outcomes.

   The direct influence of the coach is largely limited to the interaction. It is the discipline that the coach exhibits during an interaction which is predictive of achieving the instrumental results and, ultimately, winning outcomes. The Model emphasizes, first of all, that coaching:

O   is a personal interaction
O   depends on the coach operating from a particular set of beliefs
O   requires the coach to create certain positive characteristics (qualities)
O   requires the coach to demonstrate certain skills
O   requires the coach to manage the process of the personal interaction.

Next, the Model emphasizes that successful coaching achieves one or more of a set of instrumental results:

O   greater clarity about such factors as performance goals, personal development needs, problems to be resolved and plans for improving performance
O   greater competence in every area that affects job performance – for example, performing tasks, solving problems, learning, taking risks and managing change
O   greater confidence to attempt increasingly difficult tasks
O   more personal control through enlarged areas of empowerment in problem-solving, enlarged responsibilities for decision-making and self-initiated improvements
O   greater commitment to personal, team and organizational performance goals and unwavering commitment to work at one's very best all of the time.

The third point that the Successful Coaching Model makes is that successful coaching always means achieving winning outcomes. These outcomes are achieved by reaching the instrumental results. These instrumental results are, in turn, reached through the process of successful coaching which depends on the coach's beliefs, the coach's competency in using certain skills, creating certain characteristics and managing the process of a coaching interaction.

The winning results that successful coaching helps achieve are:

O   continuously increasing levels of customer satisfaction
O   continuous improvement of work processes
O   increasingly higher quality outputs in products and services

○   higher levels of team development and teamwork
○   continuous enhancement of the capabilities and perfor-
    mance of an organization's human resources.

The model finally emphasizes that the coaching process is informed and corrected by the results that it achieves. Coaching, like every other action in an organization, must be results-focused. The model suggests that the information obtained from how fully winning results are achieved is fed back into the coaching process to help improve the coaching interaction. It is by continually improving the coaching interaction that we achieve better and better instrumental results and winning outcomes.

 ## THE COACHING INTERACTION

What is most directly under the control of a coach is the interaction which takes place between the coach and other people. None of the instrumental results can be mandated. We cannot, for example, just tell people to be clearer about their goals, or be more competent, or have more confidence, or exercise more control, or demonstrate more commitment. These instrumental results, which are critical to achieving winning results, can only be realized by what goes on in the interaction between the coach and the people being coached.

This is a crucial point in learning how to be a better coach. It is quite important to have a model in our minds that helps us understand what we are trying to do by coaching – that is, that we are intending to produce certain instrumental results, such as clarity, which lead ultimately to winning outcomes. The coaching activity, however, is a personal interaction between the coach and others, and it is this interaction which presents the primary opportunity for direct improvement. The specific way that we can improve the way we manage our coaching interactions is by giving attention to the key characteristics that we know to be associated with successful coaching conversations. Remember the definition of coaching that I proposed in Chapter 1:

Coaching is a disciplined personal interaction with one or more persons which produces winning results for individuals, teams, and organizations by focusing and refocusing them on performance goals and facilitating their achievement of these goals.

The very first thing that the definition denotes about coaching is that it is a *disciplined interaction*. Being disciplined means at least the following: imposing order on some process or condition, following a set of precepts or rules and behaving in a highly skilled and appropriate manner.

When I apply the concept of being disciplined to a coaching interaction, I want to convey the following notions:

1. Successful coaching does not result from good intentions or random interactions; it results from disciplined interactions.
2. Being a disciplined coach means having a clear idea of what a successful coaching interaction is and then conforming one's behaviour to this idea.
3. Being a disciplined coach means being trained in the discipline of coaching.

Successful coaching rarely happens by chance. It happens through informed belief, understanding and behaviour.

The four sub-elements in a coaching interaction are therefore:

O   beliefs
O   qualities
O   skills
O   process.

I discuss these in detail below.

BELIEFS

Coaching takes time and, for leaders, time is always in short supply. Without very strong beliefs in the value of coaching and confidence in it as an activity which merits the time involved, no one is going to invest the time that it takes to become a successful coach and no one is going to make coaching a routine part of their leadership performance.

Over the years, my colleagues and I have led many hundreds of workshops on coaching. One of the most frequent concerns expressed by participants is about the amount of time that coaching seems to require. Underlying these concerns, of course, are the participants' value systems and the pictures or models that they have in their minds about their leadership roles and functions. Some concerns about time are spurious. The fact is that leaders *do* have personal interactions with their co-workers – whether they want to or not. Sometimes they *do* have conversations about making adjustments or improvements in performance. If they are skilled in these interactions, and matters are managed in a single conversation, these leaders actually save time. They are able to manage their interactions more efficiently and they avoid having to repeat conversations on the same subjects.

In the studies that I have conducted of coaching and coaches in organizations, I can state confidently that the most successful coaches – that is, the ones who are most valued by others – are those who share common beliefs about:

O   the potential of people for learning and performing
O   people's desire to do their best
O   winning
O   the value of coaching.

The first sub-element in the interaction element of the Successful Coaching Model which determines the success of an interaction is belief. Leaders will not devote time to coaching unless they believe that coaching activates people's potential and leads to superior performance. They will not devote time to developing themselves as better coaches if they are not positive about the value of coaching. But it takes more than belief. It takes informed belief and applied belief for coaching interactions to succeed. Successful coaches create certain qualities in their coaching interactions.

QUALITIES

Successful coaching interactions are distinguished by the fact that they share a set of common qualities. Qualities describe not only what coaches do, but also what they don't do and the usefulness of what they do.

The quality of a coaching conversation will always depend, to some degree, on the history of the relationship between the coach and the people being coached. This history includes all previous interactions between the two parties. Each interaction not only exists in its own right, but it influences the success of succeeding interactions. Success of each coaching interaction and all subsequent interactions depends upon the presence of certain qualities.

The qualities listed below are only those which are *absolutely* essential. In a later chapter I will describe just how I determined that they are absolutely essential. They are:

O   respect
O   mutuality
O   concreteness
O   trust.

The degree to which these qualities exist or do not exist are in the eyes of the beholder – the person being coached. This fact is nowhere more obvious than in the matter of respect. Only the person being coached can tell us if he or she feels respected. We can, however, determine by further analysis and observation what behaviours of a coach have a high probability of communicating respect and those which do not.

Of course, each of us can, from our own experience, describe what other people do and what they don't do which tends to make us feel respected or not. We know when we feel that we are valued and taken seriously and we know why. Some of the more obvious reasons that we feel respected in any purposeful conversation is that we:

O   feel listened to
O   feel that it is easy to participate
O   don't feel patronized
O   don't feel ridiculed.

Successful coaching interactions have the quality of respect. They also have the quality of mutuality.

Successful coaching is a shared and reciprocal interaction. The successful coach fully involves the people being coached in the process. Even in the briefest and most informal coaching interaction – for example, when the coach in passing gives a word of encouragement, or expresses appreciation or gives feedback – the other person has an opportunity to respond.

Mutuality describes the quality of the interaction – that is, the notion of balance and two-way communication. It also describes the content that is created during a coaching interaction. Both the coach and the people being coached share responsibility for the content and both create outcomes which are mutually valued.

Successful coaches do not always know more than the people being coached, in the sense of having more information or having more technical knowledge and skill. But they are always very knowledgeable about the coaching process – in other words, how to conduct a coaching interaction. Both the coach and the coached often discover ideas and information that neither had at the outset of a conversation. Coaching is a mutual learning process.

A further quality in successful coaching interactions is that of concreteness. Coaching is geared towards creating winning outcomes and it does this by achieving certain instrumental results. This sequence cannot take place unless the interaction is characterized by concrete inputs from both the coach and the coached. In other words, the inputs are factual, based on data and are verifiable.

Take giving feedback as an example. Telling someone that their performance is not professional enough is worse than useless. It is damaging. It confuses the person receiving the feedback and it leaves the notion of what is professional for that person to determine. Unless 'professional' is concretely defined, what he or she does to become more professional may be quite different from what the coach had in mind.

Successful coaches not only work to make their own communication concrete, they help the people they are coaching become as concrete as possible. Coaches ask questions, they ask for examples and they challenge. Generalities are the enemy of successful coaching. Coaching is concerned with what can be managed and what can be improved. It is concerned with performance and results. It is never content with such words as 'discouraged', 'confused', 'cooperation', 'teamwork' or any other such term, until these words are made fully operational by being very specifically defined.

The fourth essential quality in a successful coaching interaction is trust. Although all four characteristics are interdependent and interact with each other, this interdependency is particularly relevant in creating the quality of trust. We tend to trust people who demonstrate respect towards us, who create a sense of mutuality and who speak in concrete, verifiable terms.

There is an historical dimension to trust. Coaches and coached bring to each present interaction what is remembered from previous interactions. However, the history affecting a coaching interaction goes beyond just the record of such interactions, because the coach is also present in a coaching interaction as a person. Everything that the person being coached remembers and believes about the coach affects trust.

The practical meaning of trust in a coaching interaction is that the people being coached feel comfortable with their coaches, believe that their coaches will share what information they have, believe that their coaches will do what they say they will do, believe that their coaches will give accurate information, and that they will admit that they don't know when they don't know.

SKILLS

In Figure 3.1 (p. 34) the four sub-elements in the first coaching element, interaction, are shown joined by arrows running in both directions between them. The purpose of these arrows is to communicate the idea that all of these sub-elements interact with each other and depend on each other.

Beliefs impact on which qualities a coach wants to create in an interaction and just how disciplined the coach is in creating these qualities. Creating the essential qualities requires certain specific behaviours or skills. Beliefs, qualities and skills become integrated when coaches actually engage in the process of coaching. Their beliefs, the qualities they create and the skills they use, determine their competency for managing successful coaching interactions.

There are many skills that successful coaches require. A number of them are specific to the purpose of a coaching interaction or application. For example, special skills are required to give feedback, to teach and to adjust or improve performance. There are, however, a set of core skills which have general application in coaching and which are important for every successful coaching application, whatever it might be. These core skills are:

O   communicate attention
O   develop information
O   convey support and confidence.

Successful coaches pay attention to what people are saying and doing and they communicate unambiguously that they are paying attention. The first key to efficient coaching interactions is that the coach hears, observes and understands what the person being coached is communicating. All of the essential qualities depend on the coach paying attention, and every application of successful coaching depends on the coach paying attention.

The accuracy and appropriateness of what a coach says and does depends on the response of the other person. Has the other person clearly understood? Has the other person accepted what is being said? How does the other person feel about what is being said?

Successful coaches develop information by sharing with others what they know and what is relevant to the purposes of the interaction. Most of all, they stimulate and encourage the other person to contribute information.

Finding out what others know, what ideas they have and what concerns they have are basic to successful coaching. Successful teaching requires that coaches know what the other person does not know, and that the coach obtain responses to what is being taught. Successful problem-solving requires that they discover what others know and what ideas they have about solutions.

In Chapter 4 I will describe in detail the specific skills of communicating attention, developing information and conveying support and confidence.

PROCESS

Coaching interactions can consist of as few as one or two sentences. Leaders perform a coaching function when they praise, encourage, give support or give feedback. These kinds of coaching application can sometimes be accomplished with a few words. At other times, they require an extended interaction, such as when teaching, solving problems, challenging and adjusting performance. When coaching applications are extended and successful, they follow a predictable process.

Process describes the flow or episodes through which an extended interaction moves from the point of beginning to its conclusion. It describes how something is produced or accomplished. In industry, the Bessemer Process, open-hearth process and basic oxygen process all describe different sequences and actions for producing steel. In group dynamics, process is distinguished from the content of a group's discussion and refers to the way that the group is undertaking its discussion.

There is a core process in successful coaching that can be observed and described. Extended coaching interactions go through the following episodes of:
1. initiating;
2. structuring;
3. developing; and
4. concluding.
The process of coaching, and each of its episodes, is discussed fully in Chapter 4.

 ## INSTRUMENTAL RESULTS

The logic of the Successful Coaching Model that I have been describing is that:
1. Coaching is an interaction. All such successful interactions, however brief or informal, depend on certain coaches holding certain beliefs and creating certain qualities in their interactions. The more extended an interaction becomes, the more successful coaches use a set of core skills and manage a process.

2.   Successful interactions create certain instrumental results. One or more of these instrumental results is created in every successful coaching interaction.
3.   Instrumental results lead to winning outcomes.

We will rarely see, within the limits of a coaching interaction, winning outcomes such as better teamwork and improved work processes. During a coaching interaction we will not typically see improved performance. What we achieve in a coaching interaction are various instrumental results which we have good reason to believe will produce winning outcomes. The instrumental results which we can confidently expect to lead to winning outcomes are:

○   clarity
○   competence
○   confidence
○   empowerment (control)
○   commitment.

CLARITY

One of the most persistent problems confounding successful performance is that people don't know exactly what successful performance is. Certainty about what is to be achieved and what is important can only be created by interpersonal communication. Superior performance occurs when people are clear about both *values* and *goals*. Coaching, as a mutual interaction of people, can be an important means for producing clarity.

Values

Organizations which have clear sets of foundation or core values which are fully understood throughout the organization, have always been able to operate with greater purpose, with less turbulence and with less internal conflict than those that have not. Having clear values and communicating these values becomes increasingly important the further organizations move from a command and direct form of leadership to leadership by empowerment and commitment. The more leaders work to empower people – that is, help them find more ways to exercise competent influence in every aspect of a company's operation – the more core values become a leadership tool.

Values which are clearly communicated, adhered to and reinforced by leaders' behaviours give people the help they need to make decisions about what is important, when there may be no specific guidelines to help them. Knowing the organization's real values gives its employees a framework within which an enormous variety of behaviours are possible, and helps people resolve conflicts over priorities. When values are not clear, performance suffers.

A fairly popular claim made by many organizations nowadays is that their most valuable resource is their people. I find this a bit difficult to take seriously when I observe such things as:

○ training being offered grudgingly and supervisors who nominate people for training, not on the basis of need, but on 'who can be spared'

○ training being offered only in the employee's own time – for example on Saturdays and during after-work hours

○ people being herded together in spaces that are more appropriate for sheltering cattle than for serious intellectual activity

○ people being treated like children with every minute of their working day regulated and supervised

○ inadequate formal and informal systems for communicating appreciation to people

○ supervisors rarely being evaluated on their performance in developing the knowledge and skills of their staff

○ management awarding itself special privileges and benefits without verification of these rewards by the people they manage.

Values don't just exist at a high organizational level. Values relevant to performance are established by every work group, team and every leader. I have already shown how leaders' beliefs – that is, what they value – affect their success as coaches. However, leaders establish many other values which become norms governing the way their co-workers interact and conduct business with them. For example, leaders who explicitly value confrontation, hard-headed debate, risk-taking and entrepreneurship create permission for, and support, individual and team initiatives that do not exist in those organizations in which leaders have not set and reinforced such values.

Some years ago I conducted a study to determine the characteristics of superior work teams. In the process of interviewing hundreds of people about their superior teams I found that people very often associated them with clarity. They were, however, much more likely to describe clarity about goals and values than they were to describe clarity about job responsibilities (Kinlaw, 1991).

One programmer described her experience this way:

> I don't think any of us were very clear at times who was supposed to do what. But then nobody seemed to care. We just seemed to work on what ever needed working on. It was a lot easier to tell my friends where I worked than it was to tell them what I did.

An engineer told me:

> . . . the one sure way that you could shoot yourself in the foot was to keep a problem to yourself. If you had even the slightest idea that something downstream in the project was going to cause trouble you were expected to make sure everybody concerned knew about it.

Coaching helps develop clarity about values. It is one thing for leaders to say that they value disagreement and they want people to speak their minds. But to make this a working value, leaders must coach their co-workers about the values – that is, give people feedback when they do disagree and, when they don't, encourage people to disagree and reward them for disagreeing.

Goals

The second sub-element of clarity is clarity about goals. Coaching not only clarifies goals, it also clarifies these goals through a process of collaboration and consensus.

Large organizational goals may be set without the direct involvement of individuals or teams. All such goals must be translated in a multitude of lesser goals which fit the direct responsibilities of individuals and teams. A company may set a goal of achieving 100 per cent satisfaction with all its customers. This goal, however, gets translated into a multitude of supportive goals which relate to specific tasks and projects. To help the organization reach its goal, for example, a particular work group might need to set goals for making contact with its customers, setting response times to its customers' requests or regularly assessing levels of customer satisfaction.

Coaching focuses and refocuses individuals and teams on goals. It not only keeps performance goals before people, but it resolves questions about goals and maintains goal-oriented performance.

It is easy to see the importance of clarifying goals when coaching teams. One of the most common experiences of teams is that they 'lose their way'. When teams meet to resolve performance problems, make decisions, analyse performance data, set performance goals and carry out a number of other similar tasks, they often go off on tangents of one kind or another. At this point of a team meeting, a leader's task is to help the team restate what it is trying to do and re-establish just how it intends to proceed toward the goal.

Everyone – teams as well as individuals – periodically 'loses their way'. I have, for example, observed many times at first hand what happens to people in a project when the project falls behind schedule or when various conditions affecting the project change. All kinds of adjustments are required, and all kinds of questions must be answered. It becomes no longer apparent how the goals of yesterday apply. What *does* become apparent is that goals must be redefined and clarified.

The performance orientation of coaching is nowhere more obvious than in its purpose to focus and refocus individuals and teams on goals. This task requires that goals be clarified. What is special about coaching is that clarity is developed by a mutual conversation that permits questions to be asked and understanding to be verified.

COMPETENCE

A second instrumental result that coaching achieves is competence. Developing competent people means at least two things. It means developing the capabilities of people and it means developing the willingness of people to use these capabilities.

For some time now, a significant reversal has been taking place in the way people have been viewed and valued in organizations. In industrialized countries and those trying to become industrialized, there has existed traditionally a three-tiered view of human resources. At the top there was perceived to exist a small group of significant people – the executives. In the middle was a larger group of professionals – the scientists, engineers, computer programmers, accountants, technicians and managers. The third, and largest, group were insignificant people who could be easily replaced. These were the people on the production lines, the ones who waited on customers, delivered the mail and cleaned the buildings.

Although this three-tiered approach to an organization's human resources is still alive in a few enterprises like fast food restaurants, it has long since ceased to be a useful approach in most companies. Just as the goals of most organizations are driven by national and international competition, and not by management decision, so an organization's approach to its human resources is driven by the same force. Efficient and quality-driven organizations have had to revise radically the concept of a three-tiered human resource pyramid. It has become more and more obvious that the lowest tier – the so-called insignificant group at the bottom – is in fact the most important group. What has also become apparent is that the whole idea of a tiered set of human resources is suspect. In today's most successful organizations, everyone participates in setting performance goals, making decisions, solving problems, creating new initiatives and improving systems. In serving customers and maintaining total satisfaction the most important person is the one who is most directly in contact with the customer. The most important people in solving a technical or production problem are those who have the most direct and first-hand knowledge of the problem.

The old three-tiered system was an elite system. Not just elite in terms of perks and privileges, but elite in terms of knowledge. Such a system could give minimum attention to developing the competencies of the lowest tier, the insignificant group. Today the survival of organizations depends on their empowering their workforce and moving further and further towards team centred structures and on to self-managed teams. More and more responsibility and independence is being invested in people. It logically follows that the continuous development of the competencies of the total workforce is a prerequisite for the continuous improvement of performance.

Coaching is one way for leaders to act directly to improve the competence of their staff. There are, of course, other strategies. Among the many actions that leaders can take, in addition to coaching, are the following:

O   support open access by individuals and teams to the total organization

O   support open communication about company performance – that is, share values, sales growth, comparisons between past and current performance, per-share value of company's employee stock ownership plan and other related statistics

O   provide physical arrangements at work to permit easy interpersonal access

O   make space for people to get together easily for impromptu meetings, luncheon discussions and other learning opportunities

O   formalize expectations about learning in employee orientation programmes, job descriptions (if used), responsibilities of managers regarding themselves and their employees

O   provide generous time and other resources allotted for training requirements.

Coaching has a special place as a learning strategy for building competencies because:

O   it is always directly related to performance

O   it focuses on the specific questions and the needs of specific people

O   it develops further the knowledge and skills of the coach

O   learning can often be immediately verified by demonstration

O   it directly affects the willingness of people to demonstrate their competency.

CONFIDENCE

Competence and confidence are closely related and affect each other. We become more confident the more we use a competence. The more competent we become, the more confident we become. Competence, confidence and performance are related in the following ways:

1.   The demonstration of competence provides self-managed feedback. Self-managed feedback is a proven motivator for improved performance.
2.   The demonstration of competence is self-rewarding and self-reinforcing and leads to higher levels of confidence.
3.   As confidence increases, the drive to become more competent and to demonstrate competence increases.
4.   Increased competence and the exercise of competence lead to greater freedom of mental and physical movement and stimulate curiosity, inquiry, learning and action.

Coaching is a powerful strategy for creating confidence. It delivers incremental learning and helps people achieve small successes. It can build confidence with the least amount of threat and failure. People learn from mistakes, but they only become confident through success.

Successful coaches build confidence by:

○   helping people learn step-by-step thereby increasing the chances of success
○   giving people time to practise new knowledge and skills in safe environments
○   minimizing the negative results of failure
○   encouraging people to put themselves in positions where they can learn and attempt more difficult tasks.

One of the recurring testimonies of what good coaching does is that it creates confidence. Even the presence of a coach can create confidence. As one young engineer said:

> My lead engineer had worked with me and helped me prepare for the first presentation I gave on the subsystem that I was developing for our project. The director of projects was present and the group's president. I was a bit anxious, to say the least, but just having my lead present was a great boost. He just gave me a little nod when I got to the podium and I did just fine.

CONTROL

Coaching creates people who control their own performance – that is, they are empowered. In an earlier work, I defined empowerment as follows:

> Empowerment is the process of achieving continuous improvement in an organization's performance by developing and extending the competent influence of individuals and teams over the areas and functions which affect their performance and that of the total organization (Kinlaw, 1996a).

Empowered people share the following common characteristics:
O   they are competent and continue to develop new competencies
O   they are confident and vigorously find ways to demonstrate their competencies
O   they act directly as individuals and teams to organize and manage their own work
O   they actively look for feedback to find out how they are doing and how they can improve
O   they solve problems and take advantage of new opportunities, with little or no referral to higher authority.

There are, of course, limits to the control that individuals and teams may exert over their performance. Having control and being empowered does not mean total freedom. The limits of personal control are, however, discovered limits. They cannot be set by policy. They are set by trial and error. Coaching can play a central role in creating competent, confident, self-managed individuals and teams, and helping individuals and teams discover what self-managed means.

Recently I worked with an organization to integrate the functions of staffing and classification into a number of servicing teams which have complete responsibility for both functions. Each team serves its own set of internal customers. This organization was a very hierarchical, direct-and-command organization. The expressed (but untried) expectations of management were that the servicing teams would be largely self-managed, take initiatives on their own and respond directly to the needs of their customers. One can imagine how many questions the formation of these teams created for team members and for their former supervisors. For several months the new roles and functions had to be defined and tested by both parties. Both groups underwent a process of discovering the limits of empowerment. Coaching played a principal role in defining these limits. Each time supervisors were asked to make decisions that they wanted the teams to start making for themselves, they were presented with an opportunity to clarify the level of self-management that the teams were expected to achieve.

COMMITMENT

In my description of the kinds of instrumental result achieved by coaching interactions, I have so far covered clarity, competence, confidence and empowerment. The final instrumental result in the Successful Coaching Model is commitment.

Sustained superior performance and the continuous improvement of performance can only be achieved through people who are committed to the company's goals and to doing their very best all of the time. Leading and managing by commitment is the only way that modern organizations can expect to remain competitive by delivering products and services of continuously higher quality and ever lower prices.

One of my previous studies (Kinlaw, 1991a) found that superior teams are composed of committed people. A quick review of how people in superior teams described themselves provides us with an idea of what commitment means in practice. People in superior teams described themselves as:

O being focused
O looking forward to going to work
O caring about results and how well the team did
O taking it quite personally when the team did not meet its goals
O making personal sacrifices to make sure the team succeeded
O being determined to succeed
O being single-minded
O never giving up.

The lead mechanic in an air compressor team gave this colour-ful description of his present experience in his workshop:

> When you show up for work in our shop, you had better have your pants hitched up and your shoes laced. We mean business and . . . . When our shop got organized, the whole . . . operation was in a whole lot of hurt. Within one year we achieved a rate of zero downtime for air supply to every building and we haven't had a single tool fail in any shop because it didn't have air.

Superior teams achieve their superior levels of performance through commitment, and so do individuals and total organiza-tions. Commitment to quality by every single person who touches a process, a product or a service is the only proven way to ensure outputs that are 100 per cent fit to use, 100 per cent of the time. No organization has ever shown that such a level of quality could be achieved by quality inspectors and engineers. There is simply no contest between organizations that develop commitment in their members and those that are run by a leadership philosophy of control and which depend on the grudging compliance of their employees to achieve results.

Coaching is an important strategy for building commitment. Commitment depends on clarity, competence, confidence and empowerment. Coaching, as I have described above, creates all of these instrumental results, but it also adds at least two other factors which create commitment. *Coaching rewards and coaching involves.*

Three factors have been proven, with complete certainty, to impact on performance. The first is that people have clear goals which they view as achievable. The second is that they feel appreciated for what they do. The third is that they are involved in the decisions which affect their performance. Coaching achieves all three of these factors. I have already discussed the importance of clarity about goals and how coach-ing achieves this clarity. Let us look briefly at appreciation and involvement.

Expressions of appreciation only affect performance when people value the expressions and believe them. Successful coaches are valued by the persons they coach. When coaches express appreciation and acknowledge the achievements of their co-workers, these expressions have special power. Because coaches are perceived as people who really understand performance, when they communicate to co-workers that they are doing good work, co-workers know they are not listening to some sort of *pro forma* acknowledgment of their work, like receiving a note of appreciation addressed 'to whomever it may concern'.

Coaching also creates commitment through involvement. When people feel involved in the decisions that affect them, they feel included in the process by which these decisions are reached. When people feel involved with their teams and organizations, they have a sense of partnership with them. Coaching is a mutual and interactive process. Coaches involve people being coached in the process. Decisions are reached collaboratively. People are helped to solve their own problems in their own way.

In completing this review of the five instrumental results included in the Successful Coaching Model, it is important to mention again how these results are related. They are shown in the model to be connected by arrows running in two directions. Displaying the instrumental results this way is intended to emphasize that they are interrelated and interconnected. Clarity affects competence, and competence affects clarity. Competence affects confidence, and confidence affects competence. Confidence affects empowerment, and empowerment affects confidence. All affect each other, and all are causally related to building commitment – the key to sustained superior performance and the continuous improvement of performance.

 ## WINNING OUTCOMES

The third element in the Successful Coaching Model is winning outcomes. The expected outcomes from coaching are the same as we should expect to achieve from almost anything that anyone who assumes a leadership position hopes to achieve in an organization. Customer satisfaction is at the top of these outcomes, and everything that is done is intended to maintain and improve customer satisfaction.

The only thing that coaches directly influence is the success of their coaching interactions. This in turn means that the success of these interactions is determined by the competence that coaches exhibit through their beliefs about people and coaching, through the essential qualities they create in their interactions, through the skills they use and the process they manage.

Some instrumental results become visible during coaching interactions, but many others do not. Very few winning outcomes become visible. Winning outcomes are created by coaches managing their interactions and by keeping in mind the instrumental results which they intend to effect.

Winning outcomes determine the content of every coaching interaction which, in one way or another, are concerned with the continuous improvement of:

O   customer satisfaction
O   work processes
O   input and supplier performance
O   teamwork and team development
O   human resources.

Figure 3.2 is a general systems model which shows the relationships between these outcomes. The model suggests that coaching is directed at the continuous improvement of the performance of individuals and teams and that coaching interactions will typically be concerned with one or more of these winning outcomes.

The logic of Figure 3.2 is as follows:

1.   The final judge of performance is the customer. Everyone who wants to stay in business knows that it is the customer who signs the pay cheque.

2.   Customers are satisfied by the quality of the services and products that are delivered – that is, the outputs from all the processes of work. Quality includes not only the measured cost and attributes of some service or product, but the timeliness of, and courtesy in, their delivery and the follow-up that is provided.

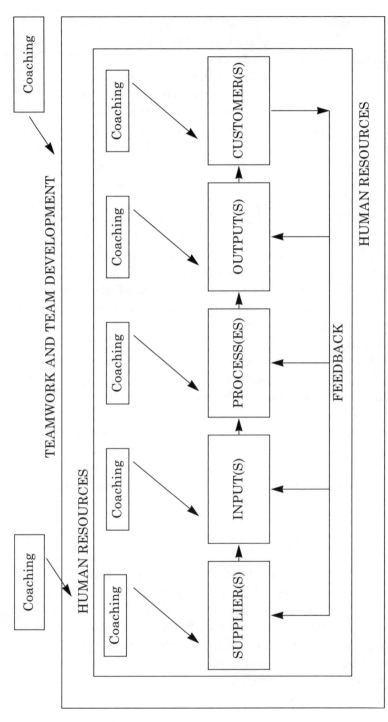

Figure 3.2 Winning outcomes

3.   The quality of outputs of services and products depend on the work processes which produce them. To improve outputs we must improve the work processes which produce them.

4.   The performance of work processes depends on the quality of their inputs from internal and external suppliers.

5.   The most effective way to use people is through teamwork and team development. Every major change to improve the performance of organizations has, in some way, involved getting people to work more synergetically – that is, pooling their knowledge, skills and experience so that the sum is greater than the parts.

HUMAN RESOURCES

In Figure 3.2 human resources surrounds the total system of production. Human resources are, in turn, surrounded by the environment of teamwork and team development. All performance improvement ultimately depends on the quality of the human resources in an organization. The environment which makes it most likely that human resources will be fully developed and used is one which is dominated by teamwork and team development.

Coaching is directed, first, at improving the quality of these resources. The specific meaning of quality is indicated by the instrumental outcomes. Quality people in an organization are people who are competent, confident, empowered and committed to doing their very best all of the time. Much of coaching is directed at improving some specific set of skills. For example, 'kerbstone coaching' describes how a more experienced salesperson improves the skills of a less experienced colleague. The more experienced salesperson accompanies the less experienced one on a sales call. At the end of the session, when they have left the client and are on the 'kerbstone', the more experienced person coaches the less experienced one about his or her performance, identifies what went well and how the less experienced person can improve on the next call. The great value of this kind of coaching is, of course, that feedback and learning are immediately and directly related to real work that is being performed. In addition, the person being coached has the chance to apply what is learned from a coaching session to the next sales call.

Coaches believe that people want to be successful and they want to do their best and bring credit upon themselves. However, people sometimes find themselves in situations in which it is impossible for them to do their best.

Besides enhancing skills and task performance *directly*, coaching enhances them *indirectly* by removing the many kinds of blocks that confront even the best intentioned people when they are trying to do their best. Blocks have many and various sources. People must manage a variety of personal problems that can impact on their work – marriages break up, family members become sick and a variety of unanticipated events require solutions. Coaches help people find solutions which allow them to manage their private lives and still remain functioning members of the organization.

Nevertheless, the blocks to performance that coaches help others overcome are more often related to technical, organizational and relational issues at work than they are to personal problems. People can find themselves unable to work around stretched resources, conflicts in priorities and a variety of unanticipated events such as the loss of key people, the failure of some contractor to produce as planned and changes in work processes. Coaches, because they can manage the problem-solving process and not because they always know more than the persons being coached, help them gain clarity about their problems and stimulate them to discover new alternatives and strategies.

TEAMWORK AND TEAM DEVELOPMENT

Teamwork and team development provide the best way to organize and conduct every aspect of private and public enterprise. Even the best use of people to produce new ideas and new marketable products is often best accomplished through teams. As one author has observed:

To the extent that we continue to celebrate the traditional myth of the entrepreneurial hero, we will slow the progress of change and adaptation that is essential to our economic success. If we are to compete effectively in today's work, we must begin to celebrate collective entrepreneurship, endeavors in which the whole of the effort is greater than the sum of individual contributions. We need to honor our teams more, our aggressive leaders and maverick geniuses less. (Reich, 1987)

There are now so many testimonies to the value of teamwork and the value of teams for the continuous improvement of performance, that their effectiveness can not possibly be denied. Increasingly associated with teamwork, team development and team performance is the function of coaching. In a later chapter I will describe in detail the special purposes of team coaching and the special skills required by a coach. For now, it is enough to comment on the reasons that coaching teams and coaching for teamwork are becoming more and more important.

The first reason, of course, is weight of the demand. Teamwork, team formation and team development are becoming the most popular pattern of organizational structure. Organizing by function is becoming less commonplace, while organizing by process and by end-to-end responsibility for production and service are becoming more the norm. The more that people are expected to function in teams and the more supervisors are expected to function as team leaders, the more demand there is for coaches to help people work in these new environments. The more that teams become the primary units of production, the less will coaching be directed towards individuals and the more it will be directed towards teams.

The second reason that coaching of teams will continue to gain in importance is that teams, especially in their early stages, go through a development process. As they move towards maturity and superior performance, they often require coaching to manage their meetings, to develop new processes for doing work and to learn to use a wide range of problem-solving and quality enhancement tools.

INPUT AND SUPPLIER PERFORMANCE

All individuals and teams are customers to internal suppliers, external suppliers or both. Internal suppliers are customers within the same organization. External suppliers are customers outside the organization. When a fabricating unit receives a drawing from a design unit within its own company, the fabricating unit is the customer and the design unit is the internal supplier. When the fabricating unit receives materials from some contractor outside the company, the fabricating unit is the customer and the contractor is the external supplier. Every individual and team has suppliers. Managing these suppliers and their inputs provides both an important opportunity for continuous improvement and the content for coaching interactions.

Within the same organizations individuals and teams can encounter problems receiving data, reports, drawings, fabrications, models, recommendations, decisions and other kinds of input which they require to perform their own work. They can also encounter problems in the quality of these inputs. Both individuals and teams can have similar problems concerning response time and the quality of materials and services from their external suppliers. Helping individuals and teams solve these problems in input and supplier performance provides a variety of coaching opportunities.

WORK PROCESSES

A work process is any sequential set of events which begin with some input and end in some output. It is the movement, or flow, of some object through these events.

An object is whatever moves through a process and is acted on or changed in some way. An object may be a report, an idea, metal stock, a car frame, a plan, a computer chip, an invoice or anything else that must be moved or modified in order to prepare it as an output to some other process or for delivery to an internal or external customer. All processes have at least the following elements:

- operations
- transport
- delay
- inspections
- decisions.

Operations define some action performed on some input – for example, what is done to change a vacancy into a filled position, what is done to transform tax data into a tax return, what is done to change rough stock into an axle, what is done to transform a request for travel into travel documents or what is done by a researcher to transform data into conclusions and predictions. Operations are anything done to an object moving through a production line to change an object from a less desirable to a more desirable state. Operations may occur at any place in a process. The first operation in responding to a mail order for some part or product might be sorting the mail. The last operation may be posting the packaged part or product to the customer. The first operation in manufacturing washers may be stamping and the last de-burring.

Transport describes the method, time and direction that an object moves through a process from one step to the next. An example of transport in a manufacturing process might be the movement of stock for a crankshaft to a cutting lathe and then movement from the lathe to the next step or operation in the process. An example of transport in an administrative process might be the movement of a travel request from the desk of the clerk preparing it to a supervisor for signature. Transport also includes the communication of information or ideas from one person to another or from one operation to another.

Delay in a work process describes points at which the object flowing through a process is waiting between steps. Delay, for example, occurs when materials are delivered and wait to enter some manufacturing process. All materials in inventory represent delay. Delay also occurs in most administrative processes at points when decisions are required, additional information must be added to a report and when signatures must be obtained.

Inspections in a process are events which assure the quality of the object flowing through the process. Inspections may consist of the review of some document for approval, or signatures by quality control inspectors in a production line or comparisons of construction to drawings and building codes.

Decisions are points in a process at which certain conditions exist or they do not. If the object in flow meets certain conditions, it proceeds along one path in the process. If it doesn't meet these conditions, or meets a separate set of conditions, it flows along another path in the process. If the set of papers required to make a procurement are all in order, the papers continue through the process until a procurement is made. If the papers are not complete, they are returned to the originator to complete or correct the set of papers. If a travel request meets the standards set for authorization, the request proceeds through the process and travel documents are issued. If not, the request takes another route.

The steps for improving a process are:

1. Identify the candidate processes.
2. Select the process or portion of the process.
3. Chart the process.
4. Identify redundancies and other non-value-added candidates for elimination.
5. Select the appropriate measurements of process performance.
6. Develop baseline metrics.
7. Select improvement opportunities.
8. Make improvements.
9. Measure and compare to baseline.
10. Repeat.

The opportunities to improve a work process are almost unlimited. The limit is determined by the pay-offs compared either to the costs of improvement or the decision to abandon a process completely. There are always opportunities to reduce delay, eliminate inspections and reduce time in transportation. There are frequently opportunities to eliminate operations, or at least to improve their reliability and efficiency. The opportunities for coaching individuals and teams as they improve processes are also virtually unlimited. They will typically require help in defining their processes, charting them, and proceeding through the various other steps to improve them.

CUSTOMER SATISFACTION

The winning outcome which all other winning outcomes support is customer satisfaction. Customer satisfaction can be achieved only if the other winning outcomes are achieved. There are, however, a number of actions that individuals and teams must take to ensure customer satisfaction. As with the case of suppliers, every individual and every team has customers who may be internal or external to the organization. Our customers are any person or group who uses our outputs of services or products. Helping individuals and teams to undertake the actions to maintain customer satisfaction is a major coaching opportunity. Consider these basic actions required to maintain customer satisfaction.

1. Customers must be known. A customer is anyone who uses a service or product and/or anyone who may have the power to influence our reputation or success.
2. The satisfaction levels of customers must be regularly measured and monitored.
3. Personal contact with customers must be continuous.
4. Quick response time to special customer requests and needs must be provided.
5. Consulting services must be provided to help customers solve their problems and improve their performance.
6. Customers must be made either members of your team or your partners.

The knowledge and skills needed for carrying out these actions can be provided to some degree by formal training. But very few individuals or teams can apply directly what they learn in a training session, without help. Coaches provide the help. Trainers, of course, can be the coaches.

I recently conducted a training programme in measuring and improving customer service for several work groups in a large medical facility. During the training session I helped participants identify their internal and external customers and gave them some experience in using various tools to measure customer satisfaction – for example, surveys, satisfaction matrices, after-action interviews and feedback sessions. All the participants gained some practice in using these tools during the training session. My contract provided, however, that participants would have unlimited contact with me for a certain time to prepare, to their own satisfaction, measurement plans and initiatives. Over a period of several weeks I gave participants feedback, encouragement and suggestions, and further developed their competencies for measuring the satisfaction of their customers. It was this coaching process which proved to be so important to the development of their skills and which resulted in their having the competence and the confidence to proceed on their own in the future.

 SUMMARY

In this chapter I have introduced the Successful Coaching Model and briefly described each of its three elements – interaction, instrumental results and winning outcomes – along with their sub-elements. It is the coaching interaction – the part of coaching most directly managed by the coach – which determines the quality of instrumental results and winning outcomes. It is to this interaction, which is the natural focus of coaching, to which I now turn in the next chapter.

CHAPTER

4

THE COACHING INTERACTION

The coaching interaction is the key to coaching success and, therefore, it is this part of the process which must be given an extended description. Only the coaching interaction can be most directly managed by the coach, and it is only during the coaching interaction that coaches can exert most of their influence. The coaching interaction has four sub-elements: beliefs, qualities, skills and process. Successful coaching requires the full understanding and integration of these four sub-elements and their translation into practice.

 **BELIEFS**

Successful coaching, like everything else that leaders do, depends on what leaders believe. Coaching begins with the coach as an individual. Coaching that creates commitment in people to do their best 100 per cent of the time – coaching that creates competent, confident and empowered people – starts with coaches who are themselves fully committed to their own success and that of the people they coach. Successful coaches all have common beliefs about:
○   the potential of people for learning and performing
○   the desire that people have to do their best
○   winning
○   the value of coaching.

Belief, as I use the term, is never belief until it is proven by action. Belief means accepting the validity of something and then acting on it. We may hold a variety of notions or think that certain ideas have value. But intellectual acceptance is a far cry from belief. One of the principal problems of organizations is that they are often led by people who give intellectual and verbal assent to concepts such as teamwork and empowerment, but who conduct their day-to-day business from a traditional leadership model of control.

I recently worked with an organization whose chief executive officer forcefully demonstrates what belief is and what it is not. The experience that I describe is real. I have, however, disguised the names.

Flavius McElvany is the owner and chief executive of a very successful engineering firm, Praxis, Inc., that was started by his father, Claudius McElvany. When Flavius talks about leadership (which he does often) and the special qualities that he strives to develop in himself and the ones he looks for in his key people, he emphasizes (above all else) being a team player.

If we should accept Flavius' words and the testimony of the banners and posters extolling the merits of teams that festoon his corporate headquarters, we would conclude that teams and team players rank at the top of Flavius' personal values. Everyone at Praxis is in continual visual contact with reminders of the supreme importance of teams and teamwork. In McElvany's organization it is impossible to forget that 'Design Work is Team Work', that 'Praxis is a Winning Team' and that 'Praxis Quality is A Team Effort'.

As his own best example of a team player, McElvany regularly congratulates himself for being in touch with the 'troops'. He takes considerable pride that he and his company were written up by Qackers and Airman in their bestseller, *Looking for Perfection*, as examples of PL (perambulating leadership).

At Praxis McElvany is known from the top to the bottom of the organization as 'Vany'. He regularly dons his 'Just Call Me Vany' T-shirt when he visits the work areas. One of the design teams gave him the shirt when he initiated his 'Work Switch Program' which required that every manager exchange jobs with some drafter or technician once a month.

Vany is venerated and feared. In all the jocular give-and-take between himself and his employees, everyone plays by the rules and stays within long-established, but well defined limits. No one has the slightest doubt that it's Vany's team. He's the owner. He's the coach, and he's the quarterback (to use an analogy from American football).

On occasion Flavius has held joint planning sessions with his vice presidents. Some years ago he started a process of strategic planning. He 'jokingly' introduced the first session by reminding everyone present that 'all votes are equal, but some are more equal than others'. He went on to encourage everyone to be 'forthcoming, straightforward and candid'. During his strategic planning sessions there was considerable discussion about goals, strengths, threats and strategies. Flavius closed the session by commenting on the 'give-and-take and the brass knuckles' quality of the session. If, however, you had been privileged to observe Flavius' strategic planning session, you would have noted that:

O   the first one to give an opinion on most subjects was Vany, and

O   closure on each topic took place when Vany 'summed up the consensus of the group'.

Vany, like so many leaders, certainly gave intellectual assent to the ideals of teamwork and team development. But this could hardly be termed 'belief'. Belief is verified by behaviour. The beliefs of the successful coaches described below result in certain specific kinds of behaviour which authenticate these beliefs.

THE POTENTIAL OF PEOPLE

The most successful coaches believe that:

O   People want to be successful; they want to do their best and bring credit upon themselves.

O   People have a desire to learn and to perform – that is, be competent.

O   As people demonstrate competency, they want to become more competent and demonstrate more competency.

○   When people are given the opportunity to demonstrate their competency, they will take that opportunity.

○   As people demonstrate more competency, they will look for further ways to demonstrate their competency.

Coaching is a time-consuming process. The most valuable resource that any serious leader (manager or otherwise) has is time. The only leaders who commit time to coaching others are ones who believe that people will respond to coaching because they want to do their very best, to be competent and to demonstrate their competence.

Another way of describing what successful coaches believe about the potential of people for learning and performing is that they make the same assumption about others that they do about themselves – in other words, given the necessary encouragement, opportunities and resources, they consider themselves to be people who will continue to become more competent. A negative way of stating what coaches believe about human potential is that people do not want to be incompetent and no sane person ever spends effort to become more incompetent.

Some years ago there was considerable interest in the effect of leaders' beliefs on the behaviour of their co-workers – that is, in 'self-fulfilling prophecy', the simple definition of which is that people tend to fulfil their own beliefs about themselves, other people and institutions. If people believe that interest rates are going to rise in the future, they will spend more money and incur more debt in the present, thereby driving inflation up and forcing interest rates to rise. Parents who believe that their children cannot be trusted will surround their children with excessive controls, force their children to become devious to protect some modicum of freedom and self-respect, discover that their children have behaved deviously and fulfil their own expectations or 'prophecy' that their children cannot be trusted.

Leaders who mentally categorize their co-workers into groups such as a) high performers whom they would like to retain at all costs, b) average performers whom they would like to keep, but could afford to lose, and c) poor performers whom they would like to lose, tend to behave in very different ways toward the three groups and discover that the groups perform in much the way they expected or prophesied. They will give those whom they judge to be high performers the more challenging tasks and those whom they judge to be their poor performers the less challenging tasks. They will give more encouragement and feedback and spend more time with their perceived high performers and give less encouragement and feedback and spend less time with their perceived poor performers. Their dealings with their 'average' performers fall in between these two extremes. By these actions leaders fulfil their own prophecies about their staff's performances.

Coaching exists through communication. The quality of communication is more dependent on what coaches believe than it is on any set of communications skills that they might use. Of course, skills are very important. The best intentioned coach with the highest expectations about people's potential will not be consistently successful in coaching others without skill and discipline. It is, however, what the coach *believes* about the people being coached that is most fundamental to a coaching interaction.

Successful coaching interactions depend upon the willingness of coaches to be influenced by the other people – that is, to modify their message, to change their approach and to use feedback from the others in order to reach successful instrumental outcomes such as clarity and competence. This willingness is a function of the coach's belief that the other person wants to learn and wants to do their best. In every coaching interaction, coaches communicate their estimate of the other person. Coaching that does not dignify others will not succeed. Coaches who do not believe in the potential of the people they coach will not dignify them.

Belief is not something that we come to without at least some evidence. Leaders who do not trust their co-workers and who have low opinions of their potential have reasons for their belief as do leaders who trust their co-workers and have high opinions of their potential. The principal difference between these two sets of leaders is that the ones who trust their co-workers, who dignify them, who believe in their potential, in their desire to succeed, their motivation to learn and their determination to do their best, have the weight of evidence on their side.

We have known for a very long time that self-managed performance, in individuals and teams, leads to higher performance. Subsets of self-managed performance are self-planning, self-direction, and self-control. All three of these had been established by considerable research as predictors of higher performance by at least 20 years ago (Bass, 1976). Recently, however, the evidence supporting self-managed performance as the way to achieve higher quality and a better competitive position has become so extensive that it cannot be seriously doubted that self-managed performance must supplant traditional systems of managing by control. Team development and the rapid movement of organizations to self-managed teams is sufficient evidence to support the effectiveness of self-managed performance (Orsburn, *et al.*, 1990; Frangos, 1993; Wellins, *et al.*, 1994).

Self-management works. Self-management depends on a system of beliefs about people which are fully congruent with the beliefs held by successful coaches. It is the inevitable conclusion that the beliefs of successful coaches are *not* optional and that they can be fully tested and proven.

COMMITMENT TO SUPERIOR PERFORMANCE

Beliefs about the potential of people and about the way they must be managed to obtain superior performance are inseparable. As shown in the foregoing section, superior coaches inevitably hold beliefs about the way performance can best be managed, which are antithetical to the traditional model of leading by directing and controlling. Among these beliefs are the following:

○ Sustained superior performance is not a function of control, it is a function of the commitment of people to do their very best all of the time.

○ The commitment that people develop to do their very best all of the time is a function of the following conditions largely created by coaching:

– People are clear about performance goals and their relative priority.

- People have the competencies to do the jobs that are expected of them.
- People are encouraged and appreciated.
- People are given challenging things to do.
- People have the chance to improve when they make mistakes.

Coaching is not only an alternative to, but is also largely antithetical to leading, supervising and managing by control. It helps create people who exercise their own self-control. Coaching helps provide the knowledge, skills, resources, encouragement and support for people to exercise more and more control over their own performance. Successful coaches know that superior performance cannot be controlled. They know that superior performance results from the commitment of people to do their best and to improve their best continuously. Successful coaches act on this knowledge.

WINNING

One reason for believing something is true is that it is provable. Believing that superior performance is a function of what leaders believe about their co-workers is provable. Belief in the potential of people, their desire to do their best, their eagerness to be competent and the relationship of this belief to superior performance are provable. We know that organizations led by managers who hold such beliefs will outperform organizations led by managers who do not hold such beliefs.

There are, however, other kinds of beliefs – beliefs that cannot be verified. We can believe in the value of something because we find it better to do so than not. Pascal's famous gamble is an example of such a belief. He said that God may exist or God may not exist. If God does not exist and we act as though God did not exist we have lost nothing. But if God does exist and we act as though God did not exist, then we have lost everything. It is much wiser, therefore, to believe that God does exist and to act on the gamble.

We also believe in something because we judge one outcome or condition to be more valuable than another. Some church and synagogue goers may believe that their religious institutions should be involved in political and social issues, and others may hold the opposite belief. These beliefs have to do with what the believers consider to be more or less congruent with the picture, or concept, of the nature of their religious institutions which they hold. Neither one belief or the other is verifiable because both beliefs really depend on a prior belief which is also not verifiable – that is, the belief that people have about the meaning and purpose of their religious institutions.

Yet another kind of belief amounts to a kind of endorsement of one type of outcome being more desirable than another. We may believe that ensuring that all people have the shelter and food necessary to maintain at least a modest standard of living is more desirable than their not having these resources. If we do, we support strong national social benefit programmes. If we do not hold such beliefs about people's having food and shelter, we will not support such programmes.

Belief in winning is primarily a belief in a desired outcome. Coaches believe that: winning is unequivocally better than losing; learning is better than not learning; solving problems is better than not solving them; working easily and well with others is better than being at cross-purposes with co-workers; and self-managed people are more useful than dependent people.

Successful coaches do not believe, however, that 'winning is everything'. They do not subvert the value of winning to the value of honesty and fair play. They believe in winning by gaining greater clarity, greater competence, greater confidence, more empowerment and higher commitment in others.

A final kind of belief carries the meaning of confidence. Successful coaches not only value winning, they believe that they can win and that their coaching will ensure that others win. This kind of confidence can only be developed over time. The more we win, the more we believe that we can win. Successful coaches, through their discipline and skill, *do* win over time.

The belief that coaches have in winning means at least the following:

○   They value winning over losing.
○   They have developed, over time, their own record of success which makes them increasingly confident that they can win and help others to win.

Nevertheless, there is a third characteristic of successful coaches' belief in winning. Coaches believe so strongly that they will win and that they can help others to win that they naturally transmit their belief to others. The people whom they coach share in their belief; they come to believe in their own ability to win because they associate with coaches who communicate clearly and strongly their belief in winning, their self-confidence that they can win, and their confidence that the people they coach can win.

THE VALUE OF COACHING

Because successful coaches hold strong beliefs about the potential of people and the central place that commitment holds in achieving superior performance, they naturally value coaching as a powerful means for acting on these beliefs. Because of this, they will energetically seek opportunities to coach and willingly seize every informal and unplanned opportunity to coach that presents itself.

Superior coaches, however, not only believe in the value of coaching, they also believe that they have the responsibility to improve their competence as coaches. A summary of the specific set of beliefs that superior coaches hold about coaching includes the following. They believe that:

O they must be available to their co-workers and must communicate this availability

O they must be sensitive to the many spontaneous or informal coaching opportunities that present themselves

O they have the responsibility to initiate coaching interactions

O they must be disciplined in their coaching interactions and work continuously at improving these interactions.

SUMMARY

The first characteristic of a coaching interaction that begins to shape it towards success is the beliefs of the coach. Successful coaches enter a coaching interaction believing in the potential of people, believing that superior performance is a function of commitment and believing in the value of the coaching process itself. A second characteristic of successful coaching inter- actions is that these interactions have certain qualities which are consistently created by successful coaches. These qualities are discussed below.

 ## QUALITIES

I have determined which are the most essential qualities in coaching interactions by means of observation and testing. We can test for the essential qualities of a successful coaching interaction by the following process:

1. Have a coach conduct a coaching interaction while under observation.
2. At the end of the interaction ask the person being coached to assess the conversation in terms ·of personal comfort and usefulness.
3. For those conversations that are given a very high assess- ment, ask the person being coached to account for his or her satisfaction and give reasons for the conversation's success.
4. Analyse these responses and find commonalities.

Another way to determine what qualities exist in successful coaching interactions is to ask people to:

1. recall a successful interaction with another person in which they were helped to learn something new, or to solve some problem, or to gain greater clarity about performance expectations or a performance issue; and
2. indicate which factors in the interaction helped make it a success.

The responses can then be analysed and placed in groups or categories.

From several hundred observations that I have made using the two methods described above, I have concluded that success- ful coaching interactions always contain certain predictable qualities. These happen to be many of the same qualities that characterize all successful and purposeful human conversations.

Note that I am comparing coaching to all *purposeful* conversations. Many conversations have no clearly defined purpose. We frequently interact, chat and converse with others without intending to accomplish anything, except to keep in touch or enjoy a chat. Coaching is always purposeful. It aims to accomplish some end, such as to teach a new skill or resolve a problem. It always aims to lead to the instrumental results and the winning outcomes defined in the Successful Coaching Model (see Figure 3.1, p. 34).

The qualities which I include are only those which are *absolutely* essential. The more obviously and consistently these qualities are present, the more likely it is that a coaching conversation will be successful. Conversely, the less obviously and the less consistently present are these qualities, the less is the likelihood that the conversation will be a success. The essential qualities which must be present in a successful coaching interaction are:

O   respect
O   mutuality
O   concreteness
O   trust.

RESPECT

Successful coaching conversations proceed towards positive results according to the degree to which the person being coached feels respected. Respect exists in a coaching conversation only when the other person *feels respected*. We can think of the person being coached as the customer and therefore the final arbiter of quality. Thus, the person being coached determines if he or she is respected.

We can determine which behaviours are most likely to create respect and vice versa by asking people what others do in a conversation which make them feel respected. I have repeated this experiment thousands of times under laboratory conditions, as well as part of my workshops on coaching. When people are asked the question, 'When you feel respected by another person during a conversation, what is the other person doing or not doing?' these are the typical responses:

O   'The other person looked as if he/she was listening.'
O   'I was not interrupted.'
O   'I was asked my opinion.'
O   'My ideas were taken seriously.'
O   'The other person didn't jump to conclusions.'
O   'I wasn't criticized or blamed.'
O   'I wasn't lectured.'
O   'The other person made it easy for me to speak my mind.'

Taken as a whole, all these comments affirm that we feel respected in a purposeful conversation when:

O   it is easy for us to participate fully, without feeling threatened
O   we feel free to ask questions and reveal what we don't know and what we don't understand
O   we feel free to take an opposing position and disagree
O   we feel that we will participate fully in making decisions that affect us.

All of the instrumental results identified in the Successful Coaching Model – that is, clarity, competence, confidence, control and commitment – are best achieved when people feel respected. Take the single example of gaining a new competence. People learn more easily and faster when they don't have to pretend that they know something, when it is safe to admit to ignorance or uncertainty, when any question is permitted, valued and responded to seriously – in other words, when they feel respected.

Staying with the same example of gaining a new competence, consider the effect that the following kinds of statements by a coach would have on the learning process:

O   'I answered that same question last time.'
O   'Don't worry about that problem, you don't know enough yet for me to explain.'
O   'Where did you ever get such an idea?'
O   'That sounds like an excuse to me.'
O   'Why do you keep making the same mistake?'

MUTUALITY

A second quality in successful coaching interactions is mutuality and balance between the coach and the people being coached. Mutuality in a coaching interaction carries at least the following meanings:

○ All parties have equal opportunity to contribute during the interaction.

○ All information during a conversation is confirmed – that is, held in common.

○ All parties share responsibility for the outcomes of the interaction.

To say that all parties in a coaching interaction have equal opportunity to contribute, does not mean that the amount of information or the length of participation by all parties is strictly equal. Sometimes a coach serves as a resource and teacher. Although, in this instance, the coach may be the principal contributor of information, this does not make the coaching interaction one-sided. It only becomes one-sided when the people being coached do not have equal opportunity to ask questions and make comments. This attribute of mutuality is readily apparent when a coach responds to a request for help in solving some problem. Only the person being coached can provide the initial information about the problem and must be fully involved in clarifying and solving the problem. There is always the freedom for give-and-take in successful coaching, regardless of who does most of the giving and who does most of the taking.

Coaching interactions are also mutual interactions in the sense of two or more parties holding something in common – like having a mutual friend or having mutual needs. What is held in common in successful coaching interactions is understanding. Whatever is communicated and whatever information is developed is confirmed by all parties. Such confirmation is, of course, a function of two-way communication. Questions are asked by one person to clarify what another person has said. One person restates what another has said. All parties periodically test, in one way or another, their common understanding of what is being said and discussed.

A third meaning of mutuality in a coaching interaction is that all parties share responsibility for the success of the interaction. The clear implication of this statement is that the coach and the people being coached affect what takes place during a coaching interaction and what happens as the result of such interaction. Successful coaching means working and cooperating together; it never means a coach doing something to another person. Successful coaches make this mutual responsibility clear.

CONCRETENESS

In addition to the qualities of respect and mutuality, successful coaching interactions also have the quality of concreteness. Coaching always focuses on what is objective and descriptive. This means that coaching interactions always move to reach a definable goal and the language used in coaching is explicit and concrete. Coaching is concerned with what can be managed and what can be improved. It is concerned with performance and results.

When I describe some of the specific functions or applications of coaching, such as giving feedback, encouraging, appreciating, instructing, solving problems, challenging and improving, I will demonstrate the criticality of concrete language to the success of these functions. Here, however, are a few examples that I have observed coaches using. Compare the less concrete with the more concrete statements below and you can easily see the relative feedback value in the examples.

Example A: *Not concrete:* 'You're doing a fine job.'
           Concrete: 'Your suggestions to improve our proposal were right on target and should make us even more competitive.'

Example B: *Not concrete:* 'You weren't very helpful during our team meeting yesterday.'
           Concrete: 'You kept coming and going dur-ing our team meeting yesterday

> and each time you left and came
> back you interrupted what the
> team was discussing.'

Example C: *Not concrete*: 'We really want to do a profes-
                 sional job on this paper.'
                 Concrete: 'Here is a model of the way we
                 should put our paper together.'

TRUST

All four of the qualities present in a successful coaching conversation are interdependent, and this interdependency is
nowhere more obvious than in creating trust. We tend to trust
people who demonstrate respect towards us, who create a sense
of mutuality, and who speak in quite concrete, verifiable terms.

Trust in a coaching interaction, in addition to depending on
the other qualities of respect, mutuality and concreteness,
depends on what is known and unknown by both the coach and
the people being coached. The quality that the coach wants to
create is mutual trust between the coach and the person being
coached. Figure 4.1 demonstrates how trust develops from
what the coach and people being coached know.

In every coaching interaction both the coach and the people
being coached have accurate, but possibly different, knowledge
about certain things relative to that interaction. (I use the
word 'accurate' here to include both the notion of complete-
ness and correspondence with reality.) Neither, however, have
accurate knowledge about certain things. This may mean that
they either have no information at all or that the information
which they do have is incorrect.

There are four quadrants in Figure 4.1:
A.   Coach and coached both have accurate information
B.   Coached has accurate information, but coach does not
C   Coach has accurate information, but coached does not
D.   Neither coach nor coached have accurate information.
The most desirable situation in a coaching interaction is that
quadrant A become as large as possible – that is, both coach
and the persons being coached have accurate information

Coach

	Coach has accurate information	Coach doesn't have accurate information
Coached Coached has accurate information	**A** **Coach and coached both have accurate information**	**B** **Coached has accurate information but coach does not**
Coached doesn't have accurate information	**C** **Coach has accurate information, but coached does not**	**D** **Neither coach nor coached have accurate information**

Figure 4.1 Trust as a function of knowing

relating to the coaching interaction. The least desirable situation may occur in two ways: either quadrant C is excessively large – that is, the coach has most of the accurate information relating to the coaching interaction – or quadrant D is excessively large – that is, neither the coach nor the coached have accurate information relating to the coaching interaction.

A successful coaching interaction enlarges quadrant A. The more accurate information that the coach and the people being coached hold in common, the more trust is created during a coaching interaction. To achieve the state of commonly shared accurate information requires several behaviours from the coach.

1.   The coach shares fully and candidly what he or she knows that bears on the coaching interaction.
2.   The coach tests what he or she thinks is accurate information.
3.   The coach is skilled in helping the people being coached discover and reveal what they know.

The responsibility for creating trust rests directly on the coach. The following discussion helps to show how trust is a function of knowing in a coaching interaction.

One purpose of coaching is to improve unsatisfactory performance. This means that a coach should confront unsatisfactory performance when it occurs and find ways to improve it. A mistake that I find managers and supervisors consistently making is that they assume at the outset of this kind of coaching interaction that they have all, or most of, the accurate information accounting for the unsatisfactory performance. This assumption leads them to conduct their coaching interaction without ever developing a large and balanced quadrant A – in other words, without making sure that both the coach and coached have accurate information. They therefore fail to find out how their co-worker perceives the performance problem and fail to test just how accurate their own information about it is.

Below are two of the behaviours used by managers and supervisors and which prevent them from creating a fully developed quadrant A:

O   They keep repeating their own position without listening to what the other people want to say or without encouraging them to explain how they understand the problem.

○   They refute the reasons that other people might initially give as causes for the problem, rather than trying to understand these reasons.

When we tell other people that we think that their performance is falling below expectations, we can expect them to justify or defend their performance. Unskilled coaches will waste time countering the justifications and defences, rather than just accepting them as potentially accurate information which both coach and coached can use to resolve the problem. The goal of a coaching interaction to improve unsatisfactory performance; it is not to prove how right or wrong a co-worker's perception is. The best way to resolve the performance problem is to develop a large quadrant A, in which both coach and coached have accurate information.

If the coach does not work at developing a large quadrant A, but persists instead in behaving as though he or she has all the accurate information needed to solve the performance problem, the prospects of a permanent resolution are limited, because the people being coached will not trust the coach because they will not feel that their needs have been taken seriously.

In this illustration of confronting poor performance, trust can be understood as a function of the size of quadrant A. The more accurate information that coach and coached hold in common, the more trust is created in a coaching interaction.

Coaching interactions are often initiated by people who have personal needs that must be resolved for them to continue to perform at their best. The relationship between performance and trust can easily be seen when we look at how successful coaches respond to such problems. Trust must exist for such coaching interactions to be successful and can only be created to the degree that both coach and the other people being coached share a common body of accurate information. The way coaches create this body of accurate information (that is, develop a large quadrant A) is by taking the needs, experiences and knowledge of other people seriously.

Successful coaching creates and maintains commitment. People are most committed to do those things which have meaning for them. Meaning, in turn, is a function of involvement and influence. Readers can confirm, from their own experience, what levels of commitment they have felt to carry out tasks which have no meaning to them or to implement decisions in which they were not involved.

Achieving and maintaining superior performance are always the goals of coaching, but coaching also strives to help create people who, through their own initiative and commitment, will achieve these goals. Creating such people requires that their experiences, their points of view and their special needs are taken seriously.

Take some examples. A coach sets out to help a person improve his or her writing skills. An arbitrary approach is to require the person to attend a technical writing course. A coaching approach involves the person in developing his or her own best way to improve the skills. The coach never loses sight of improving the writing skills, but the coach and the person being coached develop a plan that is responsive to the person's individual needs.

An engineer is in charge of developing a subsystem in a new avionics project. The engineer's spouse becomes ill causing numerous temporary problems in managing the household and caring for three children. Nevertheless, the project must stay on schedule. An arbitrary approach is to conduct business as usual and require the engineer to continue managing the development of the subsystem in the same way. A coaching approach is to work with the engineer to discover alternatives which take serious account of the engineer's problems. Again, taking seriously the needs of co-workers does not mean losing sight of performance goals. It means involving the person being coached in finding ways both to meet the goals and his or her personal needs.

 SKILLS

So far I have described two of the four sub-elements in a coaching interaction which must be managed to ensure coaching success – namely, beliefs and qualities. The third sub-element is skills.

Acting on one's beliefs and creating the qualities associated with a successful coaching interaction, means using certain specific kinds of behaviours. Through observation and analysis we can identify a number of behaviours that recur so frequently in successful coaching conversations that we may be justified in calling these behaviours *core skills*. When coaches use these skills, they create a strong possibility of a successful outcome. When they fail to use these skills, they create a strong possibility that the coaching interaction will fail in its goal. Success, as defined in the Successful Coaching Model (Figure 3.1, p. 34), occurs to the degree in which one or more of the instrumental results of clarity, competence, confidence, empowerment and commitment are developed in the person being coached.

Successful coaches use many skills in their interactions with the people they coach. As stated above, however, a number of core skills, which are so obvious and so typically present in successful coaching interactions, justify special consideration. These skills are not simple or single behaviours. They are sets of behaviours and can best be understood by what they achieve during a coaching conversation. The core sets of behaviours with which we are concerned, defined by the goals they achieve, are:

O   communicating attention
O   developing information
O   conveying support and confidence.

These sets of core skills are not *all* the skills needed for successful coaching. Each application of coaching often requires the use of some *special* skills. In Chapter 5 I will describe some of the special applications of coaching and will identify some of the special skills that are important to them. However, the basis for all successful coaching is to learn to use the core skills, and it is only as these skills are used that other skills can have any functional value.

COMMUNICATING ATTENTION

Many of the essential qualities that must be present in a successful interaction – that is, respect, mutuality, concreteness and trust, require that the coach pays attention and that the people being coached *believe* that the coach is paying attention. This statement must be clearly understood.

It is possible for coaches to pay attention to what other people are communicating without them directly and unambiguously experiencing this attention. For qualities like respect, mutuality and trust to exist, people must *believe* that the coach is paying attention. There are, then, two elements in paying full attention: actually paying full attention; and doing this in such a way that the other person *knows* that we are paying full attention.

Paying attention means more than just listening to the words that other people say. It means conveying that we are fully present and fully engaged with what the other person is communicating. We give the impression that we are not paying attention to what another person is communicating when we engage in some sort of distracting behaviour, such as shuffling papers, using an annoying mannerism, not looking at the other person or being physically manic and when we don't respond vocally or with some physical gesture.

When other people do not believe that we are paying full attention, they will not feel fully respected, they will not experience the conversation as fully mutual, and they most certainly will not fully trust us. All of these are essential qualities in successful coaching conversations and the skill of paying full attention is a core skill for creating these qualities.

Paying attention is the first step in understanding what others are saying. There are at least two behavioural elements in paying – and conveying that we are paying – full attention:

◯   listening and observing, and
◯   testing.

Listening and observing

Paying attention means listening and observing. It means listening to just how words are said – that is, noting their tone, loudness and intensity. It means observing others' non-verbal behaviour – their facial expressions, physical gestures and posture. Listening requires that we set aside our own resistances, biases and beliefs (as far as possible) and work at receiving as carefully as possible what the other person is communicating.

Listening without resistance and bias is not easy. One reason that it is not easy is that we all have a fear of being wrong. If we listen carefully to what others are saying, we always run the risk of finding out that we have had mistaken information and ideas. Another reason that we don't listen very well is that we are typically in a hurry. Time is leaders' scarcest resource. They want to hurry on beyond problems to solutions. Consequently, they are also mentally listening to ideas, retorts, suggestions and solutions that they are formulating in their own heads while they are trying to listen to others. Clues that we are doing this are, first, when we interrupt others and, second, when we don't build on what others are saying, but respond to their statements with our own statements, to their perceptions with our own perceptions, to their ideas with our own ideas and to their interpretations with our own.

A few skills that coaches can learn in order to help them listen and observe what others are communicating are as follows:

○ Face the other person and maintain appropriate eye contact.
○ Maintain a friendly and relaxed posture.
○ Be physically involved – that is, be expressive with your face and body.
○ Acknowledge verbally what the other person is saying – examples are, 'Uh huh', 'I can see that', 'Right', 'That was a good break', 'That wasn't easy' and the like.
○ Avoid interrupting.
○ Pay attention to others' non-verbal behaviour – that is, how they are speaking and how they are using their bodies.

Testing

A second element in paying full attention is testing that we understand what others have communicated. We can do this in at least the following ways:

○ simply stating that we don't understand or that we are unclear
○ using responses which reflect what we think we have heard or observed and which test what we think we understand.

The first of these behaviours is quite straightforward. It includes such common responses as 'I am unclear about what you mean', 'I don't quite understand your reasoning here', 'I'm afraid I have lost the thread of your thinking here' and so on.

Using responses which reflect what we think another person has said and which test our understanding requires some greater definition and discussion.

Reflecting describes those responses which state what we think we have heard or observed in another person's communication. Reflecting responses are unlimited in kind and in content, but they all have one common characteristic: they focus on what the other person has actually communicated and they minimize interpreting what the other person has said. Reflecting, however, is not mirroring. It is not repeating *just* what the other person has said, using the person's very own words. It is playing back to the other person what we believe we have heard the other person say, and/or communicating the feelings that the other person is conveying.

Reflecting responses will typically begin with words similar to the following:

O   'So, it seems to you . . . '
O   'You believe, then, that . . . '
O   'If I have understood you correctly you are saying . . . '
O   'What you are saying, then, is . . . '
O   'So your dominant concern is . . . '

Here are some examples illustrating exactly what reflecting responses are. **O** designates the other person. **C** signifies the coach giving a reflecting response.

O: No matter what I do or how loud I complain, I am having no luck getting the cooperation that I need from drafting.
C: Getting them to respond looks pretty hopeless.

O: We are spending so much time getting our team organized to respond to our customers that there isn't much time left to respond to our customers. Management wants us to keep our customers completely happy and still spend all this extra time learning to work differently. We are the ones caught right in the middle.

C: I suppose it feels like a no-win situation for you right now – it doesn't seem possible for you to keep management and your customers both happy.

O: All my groups seems to get from top management is a lot of negative stuff. We get blamed, even when we shouldn't be. When anyone complains about our services, management just assumes that we are in the wrong.

C: I imagine the big issues for you are that most of what you hear from management is criticism and management isn't interested enough to find out your group's view of things.

DEVELOPING INFORMATION

The second set of core skills has as its primary purpose developing information. All core skills, of course, are interrelated and interdependent. We can make no absolute distinction between those skills which communicate that the coach is paying attention and those skills which develop information. When people sense that the coach is paying attention to what they are communicating, they are much more inclined to take an active role in offering information than they are when they believe that the coach is not paying attention and is, therefore, not interested in what they have to communicate. I have distinguished paying attention from developing information to emphasize that both of these goals are integral to a successful coaching interaction and to draw attention to the primary function of each set of skills. In other words, there are some skills which are essential to paying attention and there are some skills which are essential for developing information.

Finding out what others know and think is fundamental to successful coaching. Coaches cannot teach others without knowing what the other persons do not know. Coaches cannot help others resolve problems without knowing how these other persons understand the problem and what they have done to resolve it or, at least, how they think that it should be resolved.

There are two sets of skills which successful coaches must be able to use in order to develop all the information required in a coaching interaction. These are probing skills and skills which summarize and connect.

Probing

Probing takes the following forms:

O   requests for specific information and limited responses such as 'yes', or 'no'
O   requests for elaboration and unlimited responses.

Requests for specific information and limited responses are usually referred to as 'closed'. The logic here is that limits are set by the request and no elaboration is desired. Examples of closed requests are:

O   'Did you accept the challenge?'
O   'How much time do you require?'
O   'Give me the name of the contractor.'
O   'Tell me what time you arrived at the meeting.'

Open requests do not set limits. Sometimes, of course, closed requests result in the person being coached volunteering much more information than the coach requested. Knowing the difference between open and closed requests is not important for the person being coached, but it is important for the coach. When coaches use only closed requests, or a disproportional number of such requests, the coaching interaction loses the quality of mutuality. The coached person is encouraged to become a passive participant, waiting to be asked the next question. Open requests sound like the following:

O   'Tell me how you think we should proceed from here.'
O   'Give me a description of the resources you need.'
O   'What sort of plan to you have for getting the project on track?'
O   'What can we do to decrease our costs as soon as possible?'

Summarizing and Connecting

A second set of skills which develop information are those which summarize and make connections, or integrate what others have said. Developing information is not just accumulating facts, opinions and ideas. In a coaching interaction it also means reducing the confusion that people are experiencing in trying to learn some new knowledge or skill, or trying to solve some problem or trying to make some decision.

Summary statements help both the coach and the people being coached pause in the process and make certain that the key points have been stated in a concrete and useful form and that they both have a common understanding of these points. Summarizing also encourages the addition of further relevant information and the discarding of unimportant information.

Here are two examples of summary statements.

○ 'You have covered a lot of questions that you have about using our electronic mail system. Let me see if I have captured them all and then we can start answering them. You want to know how private the system is and how to protect sensitive information; you want to know how to set up files to manage all the communications you will be getting and sending; and you want to know how to connect with the electronic mail systems of your key customers.'

○ 'As you see it, the reasons that we are falling behind in the project are: first, we didn't get final agreement from the customer about the technical requirements, and so these requirements keep changing; second, we assigned too many people to the project too soon and should have waited until they were really needed; third, we were going to use off-the-shelf components, but now this won't work because the requirements have changed; and fourth, we have a morale problem.'

The person being coached makes a connection when the coach links later statements or ideas with ones that have gone before. This also happens when the coach raises relevant questions which may not have occurred to the person being coached. When coaches make connections, they encourage people being coached to validate these connections and to look for additional connections.

Most often, when people are discussing a problem or developing some idea, they will not produce information in a clear logical or linear sequence. They will mention whatever is most obvious or most important to them. Successful coaches bring logic and clarity to coaching interactions. One way they do this is by helping people make connections in order to develop some order to their thoughts. Imagine that a coach is trying to help a team clarify how it will make a decision. Statements by the coach which help them make connections might sound something like the following:

○   'You have indicated that satisfying your customer doesn't seem possible because the customer has such unrealistic expectations. You have also indicated that you don't have very much regular contact or feedback from your customer. Is there any connection that might exist between limited contact and unrealistic expectations?'

○   'You seem to have worked yourselves into an impasse here. On the one hand, you seem to be saying that you don't have time to prepare for your team meetings and, on the other hand, you are saying that your meetings are not going very well because people are not prepared when they come to the meetings.'

○   'You have indicated that there isn't much cooperation in your work group, you have also indicated that the group has never met to address problems like cooperation, and you have indicated that you don't feel you have enough influence to do much about the problem. You seem to want to do something about the problem. If you started on the most obvious example of noncooperation, where would you start?'

CONVEYING SUPPORT AND CONFIDENCE

The third set of core skills are those which convey support and confidence. Conveying support includes all the behaviours in which a coach expresses a willingness to be accessible and be of continuous help. Being helpful does not mean making the other person dependent. The kind of help that a coach always gives is that of strengthening the other person's competencies for independent problem-solving and performance.

A successful coach always looks for some way to express confidence in the other person's prospects of winning. One way to do this is by *affirming* (during a coaching interaction) the positive attributes of the person being coached. People demonstrate positive attributes not only when they solve problems, they demonstrate them by their obvious willingness to solve problems and to work with a coach to solve problems. There will therefore always be something positive that a coach can find and highlight in the behaviour and performance of the people they coach.

Conveying confidence is largely a matter of affirming. Affirming reinforces the sense of competency in the other person and contributes directly to the person's commitment to continuous improvement. Here are a couple of examples.

○   'I know it was tough for you to spend so much time learning the new inventory system, and I know our sessions have made you put in a lot of extra time. You've certainly demonstrated your desire to learn the system and I think your effort has really paid off.' (*Instructing*)

○   'Thanks for the way you've tried to resolve this problem with your project. It has been very helpful to me to understand better just what issues you all face. Most of all, I appreciate your candour and your willingness to keep me informed. I know that it isn't always easy to draw attention to problems like this.' (*Solving problems*)

PROCESS

Coaching interactions can be brief or extended, formal or informal. The notion of process, the fourth sub-element in a coaching interaction (see Figure 3.1, p. 34), is primarily applicable to coaching interactions which tend toward being extended or formal. Process describes the sequence or developmental episodes through which coaching interactions (of any length) proceed. The more extended or more formal the coaching interactions, the more important is the concept of process or development.

There is very little process or development in brief or very informal coaching interactions. Such interactions may consist of no more than a comment from a coach that encourages, gives feedback, rewards or checks on how confident a person feels in doing a particular task. Even in brief interactions the qualities of respect, mutuality, concreteness, and trust apply. The more extended or formal an interaction, the more the notion of process applies. In these instances, coaches are not merely making comments or having brief exchanges, they are conducting conversations to teach, to solve problems and to move performance to some higher level.

I use the term 'process' to describe how successful coaching interactions develop. These interactions have a beginning, a middle and an end. Conversations are initiated, they go through a process of development and then they conclude. This development, however, is rarely linear. Conversations rarely move in a straight line from one point to another. They usually move in a circular and iterative fashion.

Figure 4.2 illustrates the following:

1. An extended coaching interaction expands the information available to the coach and coached, focuses this information and produces the instrumental results of clarity, competence, confidence, empowerment, and commitment.

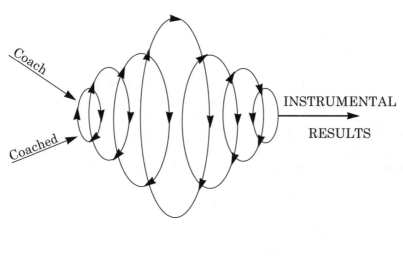

Initiating �➤ Structuring ————➤ Developing ————————➤ Concluding

Figure 4.2 The coaching process

2.   An extended coaching interaction is a non-linear con-
     versation that cycles back and forth between coach and
     coached, and moves by repetition and iteration to a
     useful conclusion.

Beliefs, qualities and skills find their application in managing the coaching process. Managing an extended interaction is
the test of successful coaching and a sure way to measure the
coach's degree of discipline. The process describes what can be
observed in successful coaching interactions. These interactions typically go through the following developmental
episodes (see Figure 4.2):
○   initiating
○   structuring
○   developing
○   concluding.

Each of these episodes has its own set of purposes and it is
by the coach proceeding through these episodes that a successful coaching interaction is achieved. It is by keeping these
episodes in mind that coaches impose on their interactions the
kind of discipline which leads to their success. Let us examine
each episode in some detail.

INITIATING

This is the first episode in an extended coaching interaction.
Either the coach or the people being coached can initiate an
interaction. What is said during this episode is, of course,
actually determined by the purpose of the interaction. Extended
interactions can serve a number of purposes. In Chapter 5,
'Coaching in Action', I discuss the following purposes:
○   to give feedback
○   to encourage
○   to reward
○   to instruct
○   to solve problems
○   to challenge
○   to improve performance.

The initiating episode can have a profound effect on the
whole coaching interaction. The coach's task is to make it easy

for the person being coached to become fully involved in the interaction and want to continue it. Keep in mind that either the coach or the person being coached can initiate an interaction. The coach's job is to engage the other person with friendliness and courtesy. If the coach is being asked for help, he or she responds with willingness and communicates the desire to help. If the coach is teaching some new knowledge or skill, he or she may initiate the interaction by communicating confidence in the people being coached to learn. In all cases, coaches avoid communicating anything that might put the people coached on the defensive or make them ill at ease. Here are some examples which contrast positive behaviour with negative behaviour by coaches at the beginning of an interaction. **P** stands for positive. **N** stands for negative.

N: 'You should have picked up how to process those problem reports from your colleagues, but it looks as if I will have to spend time now showing you how.'
P: 'I want to make sure that you know how to process our problem reports, so I thought it would be useful for us to review the steps together and see if you need any help.'

N: 'I'm on a tight schedule and I want to get this over as quickly as we can. You've been doing pretty much the same thing for too long, and I want to move you to another job that will get your brain cells working again.'
P: 'What I want to discuss with you is very important. I may run out of time. If I do, we'll pick our conversation up at a better time. I feel you are ready to move on to some more demanding tasks, and I would like to get your reaction to an idea of mine.'

STRUCTURING

Initiating often leads quickly into structuring. In some instances, the same sentence may accomplish both episodes. In other instances, the coach will need to take some time to clarify the purpose of a conversation and to clarify just how he or she hopes it will proceed. Whatever the case, coaches should establish, as soon as possible, the specific purposes of an interaction and set out just how they think the interaction might proceed. During this episode, coaches should also set any specific conditions or limitations to the conversation. It may be necessary to establish how much time is available and when the conversation must be concluded, to establish norms about confidentiality or to indicate that the conversation is to be fully mutual. If the purpose is teaching, just what steps will the coach follow? If the purpose is to improve some aspect of a person's performance, what does the coach hope to achieve? Here are some examples of what a coach might say to structure an interaction:

○ **To instruct**

   'We have some special tools that we use to assess our customers' levels of satisfaction. I don't think you have had time to become familiar with these since you joined our group. These tools are very important and have proven extremely useful. I want to review them one at a time. Please ask any questions that you want to as we go along. At the end of our conversation I will review each of the tools and ask you to tell me how and when you will use each tool. Any questions about how we will proceed?'

○ **To give feedback**

   'I've asked you to come in to give you some feedback on the presentation you made yesterday to the senior staff. The way I would like to proceed is for both of us to identify what you did that was quite effective, and then see if there are any specific things that you can do to improve your next presentation.'

○ **To improve performance**

   'My perception is that the new service teams that we have put together are not functioning as well as they might in certain ways they are responding to our customers. I would like to tell you what I see, have you correct my views if they are not on target, and then together see if there are in fact some things that we need to improve and how we can do it.'

DEVELOPING

The many purposes of coaching are accomplished by the accurate communication of information and the building of common understanding. It is in the developing episode that the many purposes of coaching are largely achieved.

If the purpose of the coaching interaction is to teach, it is during the developing episode that the coach identifies what the people being coached need to know, teaches them what they need to know and tests if they have understood what was taught. If the purpose of the coaching interaction is to solve some problem, it is during the developing episode that the background, causes and perceptions of the problem are generated through the give-and-take between the coach and people being coached. If the purpose of the interaction is to challenge a person to some higher level of responsibility and performance, it is during the developing episode that the coach clarifies the person's own feelings about the challenge and reaction to the coach's proposal. If the purpose of a coaching interaction is to improve some aspect of a person's performance, it is in the developing episode that the coach finds out how the person being coached sees the problem, develops a common understanding of the problem, agrees on what the problem is and begins to plan how to fix the problem.

The core skills that I have described above are particularly relevant to the developing episode in a coaching conversation. It is by communicating attention, developing information and conveying support and confidence that the coach proceeds to teach, challenge and achieve the other purposes of coaching. In Chapter 5 where I describe the specific applications of coaching, I illustrate just how the core skills affect the success of these applications.

CONCLUDING

In the final stage of a coaching interaction, the coach *confirms* what has been accomplished, by summarizing what has been accomplished, by reviewing the plan of action the people being coached will follow in future, tests for final agreement and tests

to make sure that there is mutual agreement on what transpired during the coaching interaction. The coach also *affirms*
the potential the person has for success and conveys confidence
in, and continuing support for, the person being coached.

The confirming [1] and affirming [2] skills are illustrated in
the examples below of what a coach might say in the concluding episode of a coaching application.

○ **Teaching**

[1] 'Let's review what we have accomplished and what still
needs to be done. We have set out the steps for establish-
ing some benchmarks for our procurement process. We
have identified the companies that you will contact in the
next ten days. [2] I believe you have a clear grasp of how
to develop benchmarks and what you will do next. Is there
anything we need to clear up before we end?'

○ **Problem-solving**

[1] 'The problem, as we have defined it, is that our customers want too many changes after we think the design
has been fixed. What seems to be missing is a clearer
up-front definition of what the customer wants, and not
enough customer participation in our design review
process. What we have agreed is that you will put together a plan to resolve these two problems and that you and
I will discuss them on Tuesday. [2] You know the problems
and I have no doubt that your solutions will be right on
target. Do you have any questions?'

CONCLUSION

I have now described each of the principal sub-elements in a
successful coaching interaction as presented in the Successful
Coaching Model (Figure 3.1, p. 34). I have described these sub-
elements because it is the coaching interaction which coaches
most directly influence and over which they can exert the most
positive control. It is those coaching interactions which are built
on certain beliefs, create certain qualities, are characterized by

a set of core coaching skills and which follow a certain process which have the highest probability of success. Coaching interactions containing these elements produce instrumental results which, in turn, lead to winning outcomes.

 ## SUMMARY

I have now developed a definition, a rationale, and a model for successful coaching, as well as the sub-elements in a coaching interaction which must be managed.

Coaching is not just any kind of conversation. Successful coaching is always, in one way or another, focused on performance and improving performance. The focus of coaching on performance helps define the opportunities for coaching and the limits of coaching – that is, how coaching is applied. It is to the applications of coaching that I turn in the following chapter.

CHAPTER

5

COACHING IN ACTION

Coaching includes a variety of interactions aimed at achieving superior performance. These interactions can be brief or extended. There are, of course, an infinite number of degrees between these extremes. The principal difference between a brief and an extended interaction is that the more extended an interaction becomes the more attention the coach must give to creating the process described in the previous chapter. Obviously, extended interactions require psychological and logical structuring. They must be given a shape which ensures that all the essential qualities of successful coaching are created and typically require the coach to use all of the core skills.

A coaching application refers to the specific purposes of a coaching interaction. These applications are used with both individuals and teams. As I discuss the applications in this chapter, I will be relating these applications most often to coaching winning individuals. All of the applications are, however, used to coach winning teams. Coaching winning teams requires some additional information and skills which are covered in Chapter 6.

I have listed the most important applications below and grouped them as brief and extended, although these groupings are not absolute. I have done this to emphasize that at least four kinds of coaching interactions always tend to be extended and that these interactions require the competency to manage a complete coaching process.

Coaching interactions that tend to be brief are interactions with the purpose:

○   to give feedback
○   to encourage, or
○   to reward.

Coaching interactions which tend to be formal and extended have the purpose:

○   to instruct
○   to solve problems
○   to challenge, or
○   to improve performance.

By categorizing coaching by its purposes, I do not mean to suggest that only one purpose can be served in one coaching interaction. Clearly, although a coaching interaction may have one primary purpose, it can accomplish a number of ancillary purposes. Coaching is a human interaction, not a computer program. In the process of giving instruction, for example, coaches may well give feedback, encourage and reward.

 ## GIVING FEEDBACK

Feedback is a term that is used to describe every kind of information that is returned or 'fed back' into a system so that the behaviour or performance of the system is adjusted. It is a term that relates to human as well as non-human systems. Feedback regulates and modifies the performance of biological, mechanical, structural and electronic systems. It can also regulate and modify the performance of individuals and teams. Feedback is a personal and team performance management tool. It provides information which tells recipients that they are on track, on schedule, meeting goals, achieving expected results and the like. It also provides information which they can use, if necessary, to adjust and improve their performance – for example, that schedules have not been met, that reports are not complete, that customers are not satisfied and so on.

Feedback affects performance in many ways. Among these is the degree of pride that people have in their work. During the past ten years I have delivered team development workshops for a number of organizations to help them develop teams. One tool that I use is a survey instrument of mine called the *Superior Team Development Inventory*. This inventory measures a number of variables characteristic of superior teams and gives participants in the workshop feedback on how well their teams compare to the superior teams on which the inventory was normed. One variable measured is team pride. When this variable receives a low rating and participants are asked to account for the low rating, one of the most consistent responses is that they get little or no feedback on their work and are never quite sure how well they are doing.

From feedback, we learn, compare what we do to some standard, adjust what we do and learn to do better. It motivates us by telling us how far we are from some goal and how fast we are progressing toward the goal. It encourages and rewards us. The impact of feedback on performance has been thoroughly researched, beginning as far back as the 1930s. Nowadays, feedback has gained a new prominence in managing performance as a significant element in working for total quality. Projections of future organizational structure show that feedback will have a very high visibility, companies will invest more and more in performance feedback systems, more forms of feedback will be created, and performance feedback to every person and every team will become more and more frequent and give information on an increasing number of performance variables (Boyett and Conn, 1991).

Having known for a very long time that feedback (when properly given) has a strong impact on performance, I have so fully accepted this notion as generally accepted fact that I am still taken aback by various leaders' discussions on the subject that take place in my workshops and seminars. I remember, for example, a long discussion that took place during a seminar about the dangers of giving positive feedback – that is, of telling co-workers that they are doing well. The opinion of a number of participants in the seminar was that, if they gave positive feedback to their employees, they ran two dangers: first, they would create false expectations from their co-workers about future rewards and, second, they ran the risk of making some co-workers feel left over and jealous.

Some of the opportunities for coaches to give feedback are as follows:

○   while other people are practising the use of some skill or knowledge that a coach is teaching
○   after observing other people perform some work task
○   after receiving the latest reports on performance measures
○   during meetings to review progress on some project
○   at the end of a team meeting.

The coach's job is to give feedback so that it can be used as a self-management tool. The goal in giving feedback, as with all other coaching applications, is to make it as easy as possible for co-workers to succeed. Useful feedback as a coaching application has the following characteristics:

○   The ground rules or norms for giving feedback are clear.
○   The feedback itself is concrete and gives specific information that can be used to maintain or improve performance.
○   It is descriptive and not evaluative.
○   It is timed to permit its best use.
○   It involves the other person.
○   It is given whenever requested by co-workers.
○   Every effort should be made to separate positive feedback from negative feedback.

THE GROUND RULES ARE CLEAR

Ground rules or norms fulfil two important purposes in maintaining productive human interactions and relationships: first, they establish in advance what people can expect to happen and sets limits for their behaviour and, second, they provide a means for evaluating behaviour and improving it. One of the most pervasive problems that affects human interactions and relationships negatively is that people do not have norms which govern the way they behave toward each other.

An easy way to observe at first-hand what happens when people try to work together without norms is to watch groups meet to conduct business without setting norms for their meeting. Norms to govern group meetings set housekeeping rules such as: when the team will meet, start and finish; whether it will start and end on time; and whether it will start without everyone being present. Team norms refer also to how the team will make its decisions: whether the team is to make decisions or only advise; and whether decisions will be reached by consensus or by votes. Finally, they refer to how the team will interact: whether it is an open, give-and-take meeting; whether open confrontation is encouraged; how conflict will be managed; and whether everyone is responsible for ensuring that no one person monopolizes the team.

When groups don't have norms, they move in a very random fashion toward their goals, they are inefficient, and they put the onus for enforcing timeliness, confronting people who tend to dominate and managing other similar dysfunctional behaviour on anyone who has the courage to take on these problems. When norms are established by the group, the group becomes responsible and reference to the norms becomes a way of managing the team.

Setting norms for giving feedback to others may not be a separate activity. It may be part of setting norms to govern the total relationships at work among leaders and co-workers. However, where norms are set for giving feedback, they must be set and mutually enforced. People will not do their best if they feel that they are fair game for anything their leaders want to say to them at any time nor if they cannot influence how and when feedback is given.

One of the managers whom I most admire and whom I have had the opportunity to observe over a long period of time sets the following norms with her co-workers for giving feedback. She establishes with her co-workers that:

1. she expects feedback from them and wants to know when she is helping them do their best and when she is not
2. when she gives feedback, she expects others to respond, ask questions and make sure they understand what the feedback means
3. she will never give negative feedback of any significance to anyone within the hearing of anyone else
4. she wants to know whenever her feedback is not helpful – whatever the reason.

CONCRETE AND SPECIFIC

Feedback describes performance compared to some standard. Clearly, unless the coach and persons coached have a standard and have understood and agreed on that standard, feedback becomes arbitrary and of little practical value. Feedback must be verifiable. Both the coach and the people coached must have a clear idea of what information is being processed and its meaning. One great value in measuring performance is that it can be based on measures and be readily understood.

One good opportunity for coaches to learn the value of concrete and specific feedback is during the coaching training programmes that they attend. The coaching skills programmes which I have designed and delivered over the years use very rigorous feedback processes. Each skill that the participants are expected to use is, first, precisely defined. Next, the participants' understanding of the skill is thoroughly tested by having each participant demonstrate the use of the skill. Third, the participants view a video model of the skills being demonstrated and count the times each skill is displayed. Finally, they practise their skills in a videotaped exercise and assess their use of the skills using a prescribed evaluation form.

Here are some feedback examples which contrast concrete and specific with vague and general.

Concrete/Specific	Vague/General
'Your report covers all the important points and your summary at the end is excellent.'	'Your report is about what I wanted.'
'The head of the design team called and said you were late with your estimates.'	'I hear that you are not fulfilling your commitments to the design team.'
'Your market analysis was clear and easily understood. It made our decision easy.'	'Your market analysis was helpful.'

DESCRIPTIVE AND NOT EVALUATIVE

The feedback that is most useful defines what has happened and the results of what has happened. Feedback is not useful when it evaluates the rightness or the wrongness of performance.

Descriptive feedback focuses on performance; evaluative feedback focuses on the person.

Here are a few examples illustrating how descriptive feedback differs from evaluative feedback.

Descriptive	Evaluative
'Our norm is that we return all new customer calls before the end of each working day. Your team has apparently not maintained that norm this past week.'	'It is obvious that your team doesn't care about the norm we have for responding to our customers.'
'Your accusations in our review meeting this morning that the project manager did not know what he was doing really got the whole meeting off-track and kept us from solving several problems.'	'You were very wrong to attack the project manager the way you did. You don't seem to care about the affect your outbursts have on the rest of us.'
'Your technical support on the installation of the new accounting system was timely and accurate.'	'The way you cooperated with the others installing the new accounting system suggests that you have decided to be a team player.'

TIMED TO PERMIT BEST USE

Feedback means giving information to others so that they can use the information to maintain and improve their performance. Feedback must be timely if it is to become a tool for self-management.

There has been considerable interest in feedback as a behaviour management tool. Most of this interest has been founded on the belief that the research on modifying the behaviour of pigeons and dogs could be translated directly to modifying the behaviour of humans. The closer humans function to the level of pigeons and dogs, the more promising such efforts have been!

The central tenet of behaviour modification and control is that 'behaviour is determined by its consequences' – in other words, when people are rewarded for their behaviour, they will repeat or continue it. Conversely, when they are not rewarded or reinforced for a behaviour, the behaviour will be extinguished. Of course, the problem with these neat equations is that most people do not function at the intellectual level of pigeons and dogs. Humans are centres of cognition who can decide to do or not do something, even though all kinds of feedback (in the form of rewards) are given or withheld. Somewhere in his writings, Dostoevsky remarked that human beings are sufficiently unpredictable (or perverse) that they may choose a hen house over a castle just to satisfy their own whims.

The problem with trying to use feedback as a means to reinforce behaviour is that human beings recognize when they are being manipulated by feedback and choose to opt out of the game. I am not suggesting that feedback may not reinforce desirable behaviour, but rather that human beings cannot be assumed to be as easily managed by feedback as are less intelligent animals.

We know that people want to be self-managed. We know that self-managed individuals and self-managed teams outperform individuals and teams which are dependent on traditional external controls. We can use feedback with confidence that it provides people with the information they require in order to manage their own performance. The simple reason that feedback must be closely tied in time to the performance that it describes is that people receiving the feedback want to have every possible chance not to fail, but to do their very best all of the time.

MUTUALITY

The final characteristic of useful feedback is that it involves the people receiving the feedback. All successful coaching is mutual. It is based on building a body of accurate information between coaches and the people they coach. When coaches give feedback, positive or negative, they must give the people receiving the feedback the opportunity to respond. In cases of brief, informal, positive feedback, the response may be a simple acknowledgement. However, whenever negative feedback is given, the person receiving the feedback *must* have the opportunity to respond. There are a number of reasons for this.

1. Every bit of negative feedback, no matter how brief or how mild, puts the other person under attack. The more they feel the attack, the more they feel the need to defend themselves. If they do not have the opportunity to defend themselves, they feel put upon, frustrated, and will waste time and energy in managing their negative feelings when the coach is not around – that is, they will worry about the feedback and complain to their co-workers, rather than work.

2. When people are put on the defensive they will concentrate on building a defence and justifying their behaviour rather than concentrating on listening to the feedback. As a result, the feedback will be largely wasted as a tool for improving performance.

3. Coaching that is mutual builds trust. Coaching that is not mutual builds distrust. Trust is a function of information developed during an interaction over which all parties in the interaction exercise influence. When people do not have the opportunity to respond to negative criticism, they will not trust the message and they will not trust the messenger.

GIVEN WHEN REQUESTED

Information about progress toward some predetermined goal greatly influences progress. The most desirable way to design work is so that people can manage their own feedback and have direct access to performance information when they want it and when they need it. However, even when we can control our own feedback, we still require information from others whose opinions we value or who have influence over our performance and reputation. The responsibility of coaches is not just to give feedback when it seems important, but to respond to requests for feedback.

Consider the consequences of not responding or responding inadequately to such a request. A technician at a seminar told me that one of the most frustrating experiences was that his supervisor would never give him useful information about his performance, however often he requested it. When he asked his supervisor, 'How am I doing?', the response was so vague that it carried no information ('I think you are doing fine,') or avoided responsibility with statements such as 'You're the best judge of your own work and know more about what you're doing than I do,' or 'I need to catch up on what you're doing before I can really tell you.'

POSITIVE SEPARATED FROM NEGATIVE

For feedback to have the greatest possible impact on performance, it must be as clean and free from 'noise' as possible. This is particularly true when coaches tell people that they are 'on track', that they are 'doing everything that was expected', and that 'they are right on target'. 'Noise' is created when giving positive feedback we interject a comment that is *not* positive, mixing negative with positive feedback, we run a considerable risk that primary notice is taken of the negative feedback.

I have personally tested many times what happens when negative feedback is coupled with positive feedback. During various exercises that I often use during my coaching skills training programmes, participants practise using the core coaching skills or conduct a complete coaching interaction. When finished, they receive feedback from their colleagues observing the exercise. If I do not structure these exercises so that positive and negative feedback are clearly separated, the people receiving the feedback will hear and retain a lot more of the negative rather than the positive feedback.

All of us have had the experience of some person (usually a manager or supervisor) telling us what a good job we are doing and then interjecting a 'however' phrase.

○ 'I think that you have this project well in hand and your progress is right on target, *however*, there is just this one problem that I want you to do something about.'

○ 'You have really got to grips with leading your team and all of the performance measures are exactly what I wanted, *however*, I don't think you have got all the team members committed to using them.'

○   'There is no doubt that your presentation this morning to the chief executive was first class, *however*, I still think you can do a number of things to improve those slides.'

What do we remember when we are first told that we are doing fine and then told that we need to improve? We tend to remember most clearly the negative statement, the value and effect of the positive statement being greatly reduced by the negative statement. It is not that negative feedback is not useful and important, but the best practice is to let both negative and positive feedback stand alone. When there is plenty of positive feedback being passed out, the negative can stand alone, and be used as information. Without plenty of positive feedback, negative feedback is not received as information but as some kind of attack or affront.

 ## ENCOURAGING

Another application of coaching is to encourage. One of the common testimonies of people who achieve is that they had one or more people who 'believed' in them. The dynamics of encouragement are not fully understood – there is something mysterious in the capacity of one person to convey new purpose and energy to another person. But encouragement that works – that is, sends people 'once more into the fray' – is a function of: trust, timing and meaning.

When a leader tells co-workers, 'I know you can do it', the only way these words can have a positive effect is that the co-workers trust that the leader really believes what he or she is saying. Because they *trust* their leader, they believe more in their own potential because the leader believes in it.

Encouragement is also a function of *timing*. People respond to encouragement most positively before the point where they have become completely convinced that they cannot succeed at some task or reach some goal. Encouragement works best when people are able to see a possibility of success. The coach's job is to help them see this possibility.

Finally, encouragement is a function of *meaning*. People must believe beforehand that what they are trying to accomplish has value. They must perceive not only that by making an extra effort that they can succeed, they must also believe that it is worthwhile to make that extra effort.

 ## REWARDING

In organizations rewards are expressed through two channels, one formal and the other informal. Both channels must be fully used simply because rewards demonstrate appreciation, and we know that people who feel appreciated for their work are more likely to persist in doing their best than those who do not feel appreciated. People need promotions, bonuses, citations and other formal awards. Formal awards, however, do have a number of limitations and cannot, by themselves, communicate to team members their full value.

First, their impact is often diluted because they are not timely enough. By the time they are received, the events which they commemorate may have long passed. I have heard many stories from people who describe how their awards didn't mean much because, by the time the award was received, the recipient had moved on to another job or the population of their work unit had changed. Awards clearly lose much of their impact when they are received among strangers.

Formal rewards have their value, but informal rewards may be more important because, as it turns out, informal rewards seem to be valued more highly. When I have asked job-holders to tell me about something that happened to them that made them feel especially appreciated and valued by their organizations, more than 85 per cent of the time they have identified some informal action or event. It is a function of coaching to give informal rewards. The following are some strategic considerations which coaches can keep in mind to increase the power of their informal rewards.

1. Don't forget the people who show up day after day and do routine jobs that are not spectacular or even visible. Tell them that they are valued for showing up and doing work that isn't all that challenging. Communicate special thanks when people patiently put up with bureaucratic delay and hostile customers and insensitive leaders. Nobody shows much interest in tapwater until it stops running. People usually take little interest in the grass around their buildings until they observe it hasn't been cut. As long as the people in accounting and payroll deliver the cheques on time, they are rarely singled out for special praise.

2. You can't say 'thank you' too often. In the various surveys that I have conducted of organizations and work teams, the three most serious problems that I have identified are that job-holders believe that:

    ○ their organizations and teams do not have clear improvement goals and objectives

    ○ that people have insufficient influence over their jobs, their work units and their total organizations and

    ○ they do not feel sufficiently appreciated and valued by their leaders and co-workers.

    In all the seminars that I have conducted and in all the direct contacts that I have with hundreds of work units, I have never encountered anyone complaining that they were thanked too often. Yet some people do have the odd notion that 'you can thank people too much' or 'you can overdo this appreciation business'. We know that too little appreciation impacts negatively on performance but we have not the slightest hint that too much appreciation has a similarly negative impact.

3. Be spontaneous, perhaps even outrageous. When coaches know that a co-worker has done something particularly well, completed a difficult task, produced an innovative proposal or solved some serious problem, they should express their appreciation as quickly and as powerfully as possible.

    One manager who understood the value of spontaneous appreciation, learning a co-worker's special achievement would immediately take the co-worker to some more senior manager and give a personal testimony of the co-worker's success. Another manager used to keep a series of specially made 'hero first class' medals and, finding a prominent place in the office, would stop work and award his 'hero first class' medal to the deserving person!

Leaders have spontaneously offered to share some home-made sweets, or given a co-worker a new personal calendar or offered a co-worker their own pen to express their appreciation for their efforts! One leader arranged for a banner to be placed on the front lawn of the company's main building to broadcast the special achievement of a team that had found rather spectacular ways of reducing cost. Appreciation affects performance. The potency of appreciation is increased when it is spontaneous and even a bit outrageous.

I have been developing the idea that coaching interactions tend to be brief or extended. These distinctions are not absolute and there are many gradations between the two extremes, but they do help remind us of the many different kinds of coaching applications that exist. So far, I have described three coaching functions that are often brief. In the following sections I will describe four functions that tend to be extended.

 INSTRUCTING

An important function of coaching is to teach co-workers new knowledge and skills. This function always has a limited purpose. Coaching supplements learning: it fine-tunes what others already know and know how to do and responds to specific competency-related questions. Coaching is not a short course on anything: it rests on the assumption that the people being coached have the primary responsibility for their learning and that organizations provide all the necessary training systems to support that learning. Figure 5.1 illustrates a framework for coaching others in new knowledge and skills.

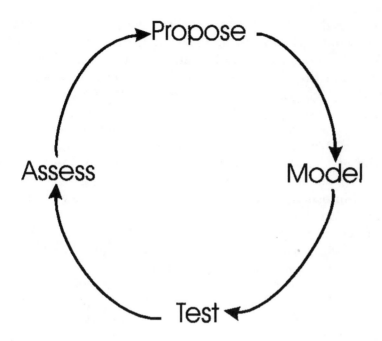

Figure 5.1 The teaching/learning cycle

A simple and proven way to instruct is to:
1. propose what is to be learned and how it will be learned;
2. model what is to be learned;
3. test if learning has occurred;
4. assess and determine whether sufficient learning has occurred; and
5. suggest what more needs to be learned.

The cycle is repeated until the person being coached and the coach are satisfied that sufficient learning has taken place.

You will remember that the core coaching process has the following episodes:

- ○ initiating
- ○ structuring
- ○ developing
- ○ concluding.

When we relate giving instruction and the teaching/learning cycle to the process, we can see what a successful coach will cause to happen during each episode of a coaching interaction.

During the initiating episode, the coach clarifies with the other people what is to be learned. Either the coach or the persons being coached can initiate the interaction. It may start with a question from the other person. Or it may start with something that the coach perceives the other person may not know and may need to learn. In either case, the coach ensures that what is to be learned is clear to both parties.

In the structuring stage, the coach decides with the other person just how the process of instruction will proceed – that is, the sequence of learning. Should the coach give some background information? Are there examples to review? Will there be hands-on practice?

The developing episode in an instruction application is the point at which the coach teaches. The teaching/learning cycle suggests that the coach will present some kind of model of what will be learned. If the coach is helping some co-workers improve the way they prepare technical papers, he or she shows them an example of a good paper. If the coach is helping some co-workers improve the slides they use during their presentations, he or she shows them examples of good slides. However, a model will not always be a picture or an example: it can be a demonstration by a coach of how to perform some task or operation – for example, how to access certain information on the Internet, how to use some problem-solving tool, how to apply some new company policy and the like. A model can also be a graphic display of some process, like Figure 3.1, the Successful Coaching Model, or a model of a superior team.

Once the coach has provided instruction on some new piece of knowledge or how to use some skill, the next event in the teaching/learning cycle is to test and see if the people being coached have learned what the coach has been trying to teach. This can be done by having the other people demonstrate the application of knowledge or the use of some skill – for example, show how to create a database, produce a presentation slide, identify what to include in each section of a research paper, or outline the steps when using some problem-solving tool.

From the feedback provided by the people being coached, the coach then decides whether they have reached a satisfactory level of learning related to the purposes set up in the coaching interaction. If they have, new purposes can be set. If they have not, revised purposes are set and the teaching/learning process is restarted.

During the concluding episode, the coach finds out whether the other people are satisfied with what they have learned, whether they feel sufficiently competent to proceed on their own, and what additional help they might require. During this episode, the coach will also comment on the other people's strengths and encourage them to keep learning.

 SOLVING PROBLEMS

A second coaching application that usually requires more than a brief conversation is problem-solving.

A problem is anything that people perceive as a block to their performance. It is anything that keeps people from succeeding and doing their best. It may be technical, organizational, interpersonal or personal.

The first goal of a problem-solving coaching conversation is to help the other person solve the problem. However, for a coach, there is always a second goal – to help the other person become increasingly competent in solving problems. As the old adage reminds us, 'Give a person a fish and you feed the person for a day. Teach the person to fish and you feed the person for life.'

The content of a problem – that is, its particular subject, background and limiting factors – has infinite variability. What is stable and consistent in solving problems in an interpersonal interaction is the *process*. The core coaching process (Figure 4.2, p. 93) provides the structure for all extended coaching interactions, including problem-solving. The most critical factor in helping co-workers solve their performance-related problems is not for the coach to be an expert on the content of every problem presented (a patently obvious impossibility), but to be an expert in managing the process of solving problems. Exactly what managing a problem-solving interaction is becomes apparent when we relate problem-solving to the four episodes in the core coaching process and the core skills which are required to manage the process. Figure 5.2 displays the goals of a problem-solving interaction, the core skills required to conduct the inter-action, special problem-solving skills, and relates all of these to the four episodes of the core coaching process.

During the initiating episode, the coach's goals are to express interest, demonstrate a willingness to help with the problem and involve the other person immediately in the inter-action. The core skills which are particularly useful are paying attention and conveying confidence in achieving positive outcomes during the interaction. A special skill that helps achieve these goals is the skill of *inviting*. Examples might be: 'I will be glad to help', 'Tell me what seems to be the problem', 'I should be glad to see what the two of us can do' and so on.

During the structuring episode, the coach involves the other person in developing a preliminary definition of the problem, sets special conditions and limitations that might apply to the interaction and outlines how the interaction might proceed – that is, its process. There may be time limitations, or it may be necessary to confirm that the conversation is confidential or that it cannot be confidential. The core skills of commu-nicating attention and developing information apply. Also, there are at least two other sets of special skills which coaches will need to use, *problem definition* and *process definition*. Here are two examples of what a coach might say to structure a problem-solving interaction.

○   'I have a crisis that has come up and, if we don't finish today, I may have to continue our conversation tomor-row, but let's see how far we can get. The way you see the problem is that our salespeople are not completing their daily sales reports regularly or accurately. You've reminded them, cautioned them and have not seen much change. Why don't we first see if we can identify how many reasons there are that keep the salespeople from completing the reports and then see how many ideas we can generate for making it as easy and rewarding as we can for them to complete the reports?'

○   'So your concern is that the training rooms are not always fully ready for use. Sometimes they are not unlocked in the morning on time and, when they are unlocked, they are not

EPISODES	COACH'S GOALS	CORE SKILLS	SPECIAL SKILLS
Initiating	Interest Willingness Involvement	Communicating attention Conveying support and confidence	Inviting
Structuring	Preliminary definition of problem Set special conditions or limitations	Communicating attention Developing information	Problem definition Process definition
Developing	Mutual understanding of the problem Mutual understanding of the implications of the problem Mutual understanding of the causes of the problem Solution strategies Mutual follow-up plans	Communicating attention Developing information	Resourcing
Concluding	Agreement on what has been accomplished Agreement on what is to be done Confidence Commitment	Communicating attention Developing information Conveying support and confidence	Confirming Affirming

Figure 5.2 Solving problems

always set up the way our trainers have requested them to be. Let's look first at what you have done to solve the problem, why these solutions may not have worked, and then figure out together new strategies that we might test.'

During the developing episode of a problem-solving interaction, the coach's goals are to build mutual understanding of the problem, to build mutual understanding of the implications and causes of the problem define alternative strategies to use to solve the problem and design a follow-up plan to solve the problem.

Paying attention is a set of skills that is pervasive and has relevance to all the episodes in the coaching process. The skills for developing information are the ones which are essential for achieving the goals during the developing episode (Chapter 4). You will remember that these are skills which probe and which summarize and connect.

One special skill that comes into play in the developing episode is that of *resourcing*. Coaches have ideas, information and experience which they make available to help others clarify what they need to do and how to do it. Coaching is not non-directive counselling, in which the total burden of finding a solution to a problem is the client's. Coaching is a mutual interaction and, applied to solving problems, it is a mutual problem-solving interaction. The coach will always, however, give the person being coached every opportunity to clarify his or her own problems and find his or her own solutions to these problems, but the goal is to solve the problem; it is not to practise therapy.

During the concluding episode of a problem-solving interaction, the coach's goals are to reach agreement on what has been accomplished during the interaction and what the other person will do – that is, his or her plans to follow up the interaction and take personal action to solve the problem. All the core skills are relevant to this phase, and there are at least two special skills that are useful – *confirming* and *affirming*.

Confirming skills are those which summarize and repeat what has transpired so that the coach and person being coached agree on what has been done and what will be done. The general pattern for confirming is 'We have covered X, we have agreed on Y, and we have agreed that you will do Z'.

Affirming describes that part of an interaction in which a coach reinforces some strength that the other person has actually or potentially demonstrated. Affirming creates positive expectations by reinforcement. The content of the affirmation can come from what a person has done or will do, before and after the coaching interaction, and from behaviour demonstrated during a coaching interaction. Here are two examples:

O   It wasn't easy for you to spend so much time learning the new information system and I know these sessions with me have added a lot to your work load. But you have really worked hard and I have every confidence that you will be teaching others about the system in no time at all.
O   Thanks for the way you tried to solve the scheduling problem with your project. It has been very helpful to me to understand better just what issues you face. Most of all, I appreciate how willing you've been to consider every possible reason for the delays. With the plans you've made, I have no doubt that you and your team will make up the time lost.

 ## CHALLENGING

Coaches are not as interested in average performance and maintaining performance as they are in superior performance and the continuous improvement of performance. The third principal application of extended coaching interactions is to challenge people to go beyond their current levels of responsibility, competency and performance, and to move to new and higher planes.

Challenging people to attempt more difficult tasks tends to be positively received by them when coaches incorporate the following in their challenge:

O   honesty and true challenge
O   value to the other person
O   clearly defined risks and pay-offs and
O   good reasons for assuming that the challenge can be met.

When we fit the challenging application to the core coaching process, it will flow as follows.

○ **Initiating.** The coach expresses confidence in what the person has done and describes the new challenge.

○ **Structuring.** The coach indicates a desire to make sure that the other person understands the challenge, to get his or her reaction to the challenge, and to make sure he or she understands the potential risks and pay-offs.

○ **Developing.** The coach responds to the other person's reaction. The other person may have doubts and reservations. The coach uses the reaction to develop new information and mutual understanding of the challenge, its risks and its pay-offs.

○ **Concluding.** The coach reviews what has been discussed, ensures agreement, expresses confidence in the other person, ensures support and ensures agreement on the next steps.

 ## IMPROVING PERFORMANCE

The most difficult coaching application is improving performance. This application is similar to giving negative feedback. The differences are that I have used feedback to describe brief interactions which, when negative, are not so negative that they create much emotional reaction. Interactions to improve performance apply to interactions which tackle a performance problem of some significance, which may encounter a defensive reaction and which require time. There are a number of reasons that make improving performance application the most difficult of all the coaching applications.

1. Often, when we have confronted people about their less than satisfactory performance, they have reacted quite negatively and we had an unhappy experience.

2. Because we fear confronting people about their negative performance, we will often put the task off until the problem has become even more complicated and more difficult to manage than it would have been if tackled in a timely way.

3. Because of our discomfort about confronting negative performance, we often couple it with some positive feedback. As a result, we create a special problem by first preparing the other person to receive positive information and then following it with negative information – rather like taking someone up a flight of stairs and then dropping them to the ground!

4. Because we want to avoid all thoughts of confronting others, we don't tackle the issue head-on and develop the necessary competencies for this coaching interaction.

Figure 5.3 displays the goals of a performance improvement interaction, the core skills required to conduct the interaction and special skills, all related to the four episodes of the core coaching process. You will notice that the process of improving performance is very similar to that for solving problems. The most desirable condition is, of course, to make an interaction to improve performance a problem-solving conversation in which the coach and the people being coached reach agreement on the nature of the negative performance and how to remedy it.

The principal differences between an interaction to improve performance and an interaction to solve problems are as follows:

O   Interactions to improve performance are initiated by the coach; problem-solving interactions are initiated by others.

O   Interactions to improve performance start with the coach's perception of the problem; problem-solving interactions start with perceptions of others.

O   Interactions to improve performance most often encounter some kind of negative response or defensiveness on the part of the person confronted; problem-solving interactions do not usually create such negative responses.

During the initiating episode of a coaching interaction to improve performance, the coach's job is to indicate, in as friendly a manner as possible, that the conversation is about a performance problem which the coach wants to put right and which the coach believes the other person wants to, and can, remedy.

During the structuring episode, the coach describes the process that he or she wants to follow and gives his or her perception of the problem. Points about the process that the coach will emphasize can be illustrated with the following general example:

EPISODES	COACH'S GOALS	CORE SKILLS	SPECIAL SKILLS
Initiating	Purpose of conversation Willingness	Communicating attention Conveying support and confidence	
	Involvement		
Structuring	Preliminary definition of problem	Communicating attention	Assert
	Set special conditions or limitations	Developing information	Process definition
Developing	Mutual understanding of the problem	Communicating attention	Resourcing
	Mutual understanding of the implications of the problem	Developing information	Respond to the response
	Mutual understanding of the causes of the problem Solution strategies Mutual follow-up plans		
Concluding	Agreement on what has been accomplished	Communicating attention	Confirming
	Agreement on what is to be done	Developing information	Affirming
	Confidence	Conveying support and confidence	
	Commitment		

Figure 5.3 Improving performance

'Thanks for coming in. I want to talk about a problem that I see developing. I would like to tell you what I see, get your reaction, and then determine together if we have a problem, what kind of a problem we have, and if something needs to be done, what that something is. It appears that we are heading for an overrun on your project's budget. If this is the case, I would like to work with you to see if we can head the problem off.'

During the developing episode, the coach explores fully the other person's reactions and perception of the problem, develops a mutual agreement about the nature of the problem (assuming there is one), agrees how to solve it, and agrees to achieve that end. There are two special skills required during the developing episode. These are: *asserting* and *responding* to the response.

Asserting has the following characteristics:

1. It is a concrete statement of what the coach sees as a problem.
2. It describes the consequences of the problem – that is, why it is important.
3. It describes a primary interest in solving the problem and not finding fault.

Here are some examples of what an asserting statement might look like. The bracket number in front of each part of each statement corresponds to the numbered characteristics above. Note that there is no set order in which the three elements must be included.

[1] 'I think we agreed that you would clear up the backlog of service requests by the first of this month. We have passed the first of the month and there is still a considerable backlog. [2] We are losing customers because we are not responding to their service requests. This is a problem that we must put right. [3] I want to work with you and figure out how we can eliminate the backlog as quickly as possible.'

[2] 'We seem to still be falling behind our projected schedule for installing the hard wire for our new network system. We are not just losing time – we are running over our projected

costs and holding up the people who are coming behind with the new hardware and software installations. [1] According to your last estimate, we are now at least a week behind the last schedule you gave me. [3] Let's put our heads together and do whatever we need to do to get the project back on track.'

Once the coach has made an assertion of what he or she considers to be the performance problem, the person being coached will respond in some way. The second special skill is to respond to the other's response by turning the response into a process of developing information and understanding.

The other person may react defensively, aggressively or passively. He or she will try to protect themselves in some way. Protective behaviour is perfectly natural – few of us will not make some attempt to protect ourselves when we feel under attack. Most of us will always find causes external to ourselves for our failures. The key to successful confrontation is to accept such behaviour as natural and expected. The skilled coach will not contradict or take exception to the content of the other's response. The successful coach will use the two sets of core skills, communicating attention and developing information, to explore fully the other person's perception of the problem.

The sequence the unskilled coach will follow is:

Unskilled coach	Person being coached
1. States his or her perception of the performance problem. Does not use a clean asserting statement that focuses on remedying the problem, but focuses on the failure of the other person.	2. Responds in some way to protect self.
3. Takes issue with the other person's response – that is, contradicts, disagrees, or ignores and just restates problem.	4. Tries to give his or her perception of problem. Tries to be heard. Does not feel respected. Will not actively seek for mutual solution.

The sequence the skilled coach will follow is:

Skilled coach	Person being coached
1. Asserts perception of problem and focuses on remedying the problem and not finding fault.	2. Responds in some way to protect self.
3. Responds to the response with skills that communicate attention and develop information. Does not take exception to response of the other person.	4. Feels respected. Participates in developing a full description of the problem, a mutual understanding of the problem and a mutual solution.

The concluding episode follows the same pattern as the concluding episode in solving problems. What has happened, of course, is that the skilled coach has turned the conversation into a problem-solving interaction. During this phase the coach confirms what has been discussed, what agreements have been reached and what the other person will do to remedy the problem. As with any problem-solving conversation, the coach gives the other person every opportunity to develop his or her own solution to the problem.

 CONCLUSION

I have now described the principal coaching applications. I have suggested that certain applications are often brief and certain others are extended. The brief applications are: to give feedback, to encourage and to reward. The extended applications are: to instruct, to solve problems, to challenge and to improve performance.

Everything that I have described about coaching is applicable to coaching both individuals and teams. The definition of coaching, the Successful Coaching Model, and my description of the principal coaching applications not only apply to coaching winning individuals, but also to coaching winning teams. In the case of teams, however, successful coaches require some additional information and skills. Coaching winning teams is therefore the subject of the following chapter.

6

COACHING WINNING TEAMS

As organizations structure themselves so that the primary units of production are not individuals but teams, we can expect the role of coaching teams to become an activity that is even more important than coaching individuals. As with coaching individuals, coaching teams is a leadership function, not a leadership role.

THE TEAM COACH

Anyone who has the skills and opportunity can coach. Coaching is a required activity for everyone who occupies a formal or assigned leadership position, but it is also a potential activity that anyone can, and should, perform. Everyone has opportunities to function as a leader. The more empowered an organization becomes, the more each person will, in fact, take on leadership responsibilities because he or she possesses some special competence or has a special opportunity. Teams present such a special opportunity. On successful teams, leadership flows among the members. Authority is vested in the team. Leadership is exercised through competence and not through position. Teams present members with an unlimited number of opportunities to function as leaders and, therefore, with unlimited opportunities to function as coaches to other team members.

Teams may or may not have a formally designated supervisor or leader. The more independent and self-managed teams become, the less likely it is that they will have designated leaders. With or without designated leaders, every member of a team will perform leadership functions. Each time members take the initiative in helping their team learn, solve problems, improve meetings, set goals, plan performance strategies and perform any performance task, these members act as leaders.

Good leaders coach and good team members do the same. Good team members will find opportunities to employ all of the coaching applications that I have already identified. They will help their teams by:

○ giving feedback
○ encouraging
○ rewarding
○ instructing
○ solving problems
○ challenging
○ improving performance.

 ## SPECIAL KNOWLEDGE AND SKILLS FOR COACHING TEAMS

The successful coaching of teams requires that the same beliefs be operative, the same qualities be created, the same skills be used and the same process be followed as those that apply when coaching individuals. In many instances, of course, team members may be coached as individuals.

What a team coach does and what a team coach must know can be summarized as follows:

1. A team coach requires the same knowledge and skills as a person who coaches individuals. A team coach must understand, and be able to use, all of the competencies suggested in the Successful Coaching Model.

2. A team coach must have the special knowledge and skills for helping a team manage its meetings.

3. A team coach must have a set of additional knowledge and skills for using all of the coaching applications with

teams. They must be able to give feedback, encourage, reward, instruct, solve problems, challenge and improve performance with teams.

4.   A team coach must be able to help a team use special team problem-solving tools.

I have already covered the first set of knowledge and skills in the previous chapters. In the sections that follow I will discuss the other three sets of knowledge and skills which apply specifically to coaching teams. First, I will describe what a coach must know and be able to do to help a team manage its meetings. Second, I will discuss the coaching applications as applied to teams. Third, I will present an overview of a few of the basic team problem-solving tools that a coach must be able to use and teach team members to use.

SKILLS TO HELP TEAMS MANAGE TEAM MEETINGS

There are two prerequisites for coaching a team. First, the team must be in a meeting. Second, the team must function as an efficient and effective group during its meeting. One of the potential problems that coaches of teams face is that the team may not manage its meeting well enough to achieve any significant outcomes, such as learning, solving problems or improving performance. There are times when the focus of coaching a team must be on the way the team runs its meetings.

When a coach is involved with one individual, the interaction is between the coach and the individual. When a coach is involved with a team, the interaction becomes more complicated and exits in at least three dimensions:

1.   interactions between the coach and individuals in the team;
2.   interactions between the coach and the whole team; and
3.   interactions among the members of the team.

One way to understand just what special knowledge and skills are required for coaching a team is to imagine circumstances in which coaching a team will be easy and in which it will be difficult. Coaching a team will be easiest when the team members interact easily and well, when they adhere to a set of commonly understood norms, when they stay focused on their tasks, and when they use all of their members' resources. In short, it is easiest to coach a team when the team functions as a single, fully integrated unit.

The basic tool that a coach needs to help a team run its meetings is a knowledge of the key variables that affect meetings and how to use this knowledge to help a team improve them. The key variables which affect the success of a team meeting are:

○   how the meeting is structured
○   how well resources are identified and used
○   how well team members communicate
○   how well the team evaluates its performance during meetings.

STRUCTURE

The structure of a meeting includes everything that a team does to help it make explicit the responsibilities of members for a meeting and how members will function during a meeting. Structuring a team does not mean enacting a body of rules, like those required for congresses and parliaments and other large meetings, which can inhibit free and easy interaction. It means helping a team conduct its meetings in a purposeful, rational and fully aware manner. The specific things that teams need to do to structure their meetings, and the things which a team coach will help a team do are:

○   set norms
○   clarify roles and responsibilities
○   set clear meeting outcomes and agendas
○   set clear process steps for making decisions and solving problems.

Norms

Norms are the rules or expectations that teams set to govern the behaviour of team members before, during and after a meeting. They serve two functions: they state how the team will function and they serve as a tool to assess how a team did function. Here is a typical set of norms that a team might use to manage its meetings:

○ All members will be notified, in a timely manner, of the time, place, purpose and agenda of each meeting.
○ Members will always be fully prepared for a meeting.
○ Meetings will start and end on time.
○ Members will remain present during the whole meeting.
○ All decisions will be made by consensus.
○ There will be no criticism of each other.
○ Every member will participate fully.
○ No one person will dominate a meeting.
○ A record will be kept of the topics covered and the decisions made at each meeting.
○ A record of the topics covered and decisions made will be sent to each member within 24 hours after a meeting.

Roles and responsibilities

Clarifying roles and responsibilities also help structure a team. The kinds of things that a team should make explicit include:

○ whether there will be a leader and, if so, the leader's responsibilities
○ whether there will be a facilitator and, if so, the facilitator's responsibilities
○ the role of appointed leaders like supervisors and managers during a meeting
○ the appointment of people with special responsibilities – for example, keeping a record of team meetings.

Outcomes and agendas

A third way to help structure a meeting is to ensure that the meeting has a clear set of outcomes that it intends to produce and a clear agenda that it will follow. Setting outcomes and agendas before a meeting and clarifying these at the outset of a meeting does not mean that a team cannot deviate from these. The reason for doing this is to keep the team aware of its purposes and, then, if it wants to take another path, it can make the change consciously.

It is always useful to state, whenever possible, what a team is to produce during a meeting, rather than simply state the topics to be covered. Performance can be measured more accurately against expected outcomes than against a set of topics.

Process steps

One way in which teams lose direction during a meeting is by either failing to set a sequence for solving some problem or making some decision or, if they have set such a sequence, by failing to follow it. Process steps can be of a general nature and have a wide application to any problem-solving process, or they may be very specific and apply to the use of some special problem-solving tool, like the nominal group technique.

If a coach observes a team beginning to solve a problem without agreeing on the steps for the team to follow, the coach should help the team agree on a set of such steps. Steps that can be applied to most problem-solving processes include:
1.   Define the problem in terms that allow it to be remedied.
2.   Establish success criteria to identify when problem is remedied.
3.   Identify the causes of the problem.
4.   Generate alternative strategies for solving the problem.
5.   Develop an action plan.
6.   Implement the action plan.
7.   Assess success.

All rational problem-solving tools follow a set of steps. One of the most common such tool is brainstorming which is often used by teams without following the required steps. As a result, teams often do not obtain the benefit from this simple, but powerful, tool. I have set out these steps in the section entitled, 'Special Team Problem-Solving Tools' (see pages 149–151). The coach's job is to help a team follow the required steps while it uses any of the many team problem-solving tools.

SKILLS FOR USING THE COACHING
APPLICATIONS WITH TEAMS

A second set of special skills required by a team coach are ones related to the several coaching applications that we have identified and discussed in Chapter 5 and which are reviewed briefly below.

○ **Giving feedback.** Feedback is a performance management tool. It tells recipients that they are on track, on schedule, meeting goals, achieving expected results and so on. It also provides information which they can use to adjust and improve their performance – that is, that schedules have not been met, that reports are not complete, that customers are not satisfied and so on.

○ **Encouraging.** People experience setbacks and disappointments. They can lose heart and the confidence that they can succeed. Coaches can use the power of their trusting relationship to rally people's strength and will to make yet another attempt to perform some task or reach some goal.

○ **Rewarding.** People work hardest and best when they feel appreciated. Successful coaches are quicker to give praise than find fault. They are sensitive to the many opportunities for giving concrete, timely, and innovative 'thanks' to others.

○ **Instructing.** An important coaching function is to teach co-workers new knowledge and skills. Coaching supplements other forms of learning. It fine-tunes what others already know and know how to do. It responds to specific competency-related needs.

○ **Solving problems.** Coaches make it as easy as possible for individuals and teams to do their best. Sometimes this means removing problems. Problems are anything which blocks performance.

○ **Challenging.** Coaches are not as interested in average performance and maintaining performance as they are in superior performance and its continuous improvement. A principal application of coaching is to challenge people to go beyond their current levels of responsibility, competency and performance and to move to new and higher planes.

○ **Improving performance.** All coaching interactions are intended to improve performance. Sometimes, however, coaches must respond to performance which is below expectations. These interactions tend to be confrontational and will usually create some negative emotional reaction on the part of the persons being coached.

Now that we have reviewed the applications of coaching, let us examine each of these in some detail as they would be employed with teams, rather than with individuals. In describing each of the coaching functions as applied to teams, I will not repeat what I have already said in previous chapters. I assume that everything that I have described about employing the coaching applications with individuals also applies to employing them with teams. I will only give additional information that applies specifically to teams.

GIVING FEEDBACK

In discussing the use of the various coaching applications with teams, I always assume that the person coaching has been accepted as a coach. This acceptance may derive from the designated leadership role the person occupies or it may derive from the demonstrated success that a person has had as a team coach.

In Chapter 5 I listed the characteristics which apply when coaches give feedback. These characteristics also apply to feedback given to teams.

Coaches will give feedback to teams concerning all the winning outcomes listed in the Successful Coaching Model (Figure 3.1, p. 34). One of the outcomes listed has special relevance to teams – teamwork and team development. The coach helps the team answer the question, 'How well is the team developing itself as a team?'.

To give feedback on team development assumes that the team has first set itself some standards or goals for development. The coach's first task is to make sure that the team has indeed done this. As always, feedback that is not based on standards is arbitrary, tends to be unfocused and is of little use.

Listed below are some of the team characteristics which we know to be predictive of high levels of group formation and performance.

○ **Inclusion.** There are no second-class citizens on superior teams. Everyone feels like a fully functioning member, included in the team's total effort, values and goals. Team members are respected, and their ideas and their competencies are taken seriously. There are no cliques or 'in groups'.

○ **Commitment.** Commitment is a goal of coaching and, not surprisingly, it is a characteristic of superior teams. Commitment requires clarity about team goals, priorities and values. It is demonstrated by members consistently doing their very best all of the time and their willingness to make personal sacrifices to help their team reach its goals. Commitment describes how team members feel about their teams' values and goals and what they are prepared to do to help their teams reach and protect these values and goals.

○ **Loyalty.** Loyalty describes how team members feel towards each other and what they are willing to do to support and protect each other.

○ **Pride.** Pride, in the context of superior teams, differs from the common use of the term. Pride among team members of superior teams means *pride in the team and its accomplishments*. Individual pride in individual accomplishments takes second place to pride in the team. Also, in superior teams, members take pride not only in what has been accomplished, but also in what members believe the team will achieve in the future.

○ **Trust.** Trust, in the context of superior team development, refers largely to the way team members accept their colleagues. First, they always accept at face value and without question what another member says he or she will do and what he or she says is fact. Second, they always believe that when another team member indicates that he or she will do something, that this can be relied on 100 per cent of the time.

This set of characteristics can be used to produce a standard checklist of items which a coach can use to help a team obtain feedback about its development. Of course, there may be other characteristics that a team may want to measure, and a coach, with the cooperation of the team being coached, can develop its own individual checklist for giving a team feedback on these five characteristics. As a guide, a sample checklist is given below.

Checklist: Team development feedback

Inclusion
- ⭘ The input of all members is typically taken seriously when the team sets goals.
- ⭘ Members are typically consulted before changes are made that affect them.
- ⭘ There are no cliques that create divisiveness.
- ⭘ Members are typically acknowledged for their contributions.
- ⭘ Members are always treated with respect by other members.

Commitment
- ⭘ Members are clear about the primary goals of the team.
- ⭘ Members are clear about the team's core values.
- ⭘ Members will readily make personal sacrifices to help the team succeed.
- ⭘ Members typically get all the information they need to perform successfully.
- ⭘ Members are optimistic that they can get the job done – regardless of the obstacles.

Loyalty
- ⭘ Members can get help easily from each other, when they need it.
- ⭘ Members go out of their way to ensure the success of their fellow members.
- ⭘ Members rarely criticize another member to a third party.
- ⭘ Members praise each other much more than they find fault with each other.
- ⭘ When one member has a personal problem and wants help, he or she can count on getting it from other members.

Pride
O Members all believe that what the team is doing is truly important.
O Members never make excuses for team failures.
O The whole team knows at all times exactly how satisfied all its customers are.
O Members are always working to improve everything they do.
O Members are typically very positive to others about their team's performance.

Trust
O When a member says he or she will do something, you can typically rely on it.
O Members typically give each other information that is 100 per cent accurate.
O When members don't know something, they will typically tell you they don't and not pretend that they do.
O When a member doesn't agree with another member, he or she will let the other member know – regardless of the other member's position or standing.
O Members never conceal anything from other members that they feel those members should know.

ENCOURAGING

Teams, like individuals, get stuck. They come to a point where they feel progress is impossible and that they cannot achieve some goal or carry out some task. What is special about teams is that they get stuck as teams. They begin to feel that being a team is their problem and that trying to achieve some goal or perform some task as a team is their principal problem. They begin to give up on the notion of team and of being able to perform as a team.

There are some obstacles that teams cannot overcome, no matter how much a coach may encourage them or how hard they might try. Unrealistic expectations created by management, lack of management support, lack of training for team leaders and members, inability to meet easily and frequently and the lack of organizational accountability and rewards are some of the causes for teams' discouragement and failure which teams are unlikely to overcome by themselves. There are, however, other sources of discouragement and failure which teams create for themselves. Teams create the seeds for their own failure and discouragement when they:

○ fail to develop specific performance goals and clear strategies for achieving their goals

○ fail to develop the knowledge and skills for successfully managing their meetings

○ fail to assume as much responsibility as they can for their own development and performance

○ fail to establish and use a regular and structured process for evaluating their own performance.

When teams are failing the areas listed above, they tend to indicate this by demonstrating the following kinds of behaviours:

○ cynicism about teams and teamwork ('All we seem to do is pool our ignorance. Just throwing a group of people together never improves anything')

○ lack of enthusiasm and interest ('I make the team meetings when I can, but I have real work to do')

○ lack of personal loyalty to each other ('We have too many drones and not enough worker bees')

○ lack of identity ('We are a team because management says we are a team, but that's about it').

The best way for a coach to help a team overcome its sense of failure and discouragement is to help it find very concrete ways to respond. I am reminded of a dear aunt of mine who, whenever she felt despondent, would start washing clothes. Her response to her despair was to do something at which she knew she could succeed and for which there were visible and useful results.

The point is that encouragement cannot be vacuous. Coaching is not cheerleading. Coaches are not fans, shouting appreciation and encouragement to their teams. Coaches couple their encouragement with practical ideas to help their teams move beyond their discouragement. Here are a few practical ways that coaches can ensure that their attempts at encouragement are also practical acts of assistance.

1. **Take stock.** Use the four reasons for failure and discouragement listed above and help the team use them to take stock of itself and identify what it has been doing well and what it needs to put right.
2. **Identify immediate and certain improvement opportunities.** The best way to overcome discouragement with teams (as with individuals) is to help them find some things that they can achieve quickly.
3. **Be a resource for new ideas and approaches.** Teams can become discouraged because they keep using the same information, the same behaviours and the same tools to solve their problems and attain their performance goals. One thing that coaches can do is inject new ideas and propose new approaches. Teams often get stuck and discouraged without knowing about, or using, many resources that are available to them.

Here is an example of what one coach did to overcome the discouragement that one team experienced. The team was put together in the training department of a large healthcare organization. The purpose of the team, as delivered by management, was 'to validate the relevance and effectiveness of all training delivered by the department'.

The team had a number of meetings and began to define how it would proceed to achieve its goal. One early problem that it encountered was that of determining just what its purpose was. It finally rejected the goal that it was given and redefined its purpose as one of 'developing a computerized system for determining the needs of all employees in the organization'. After a few more meetings, the team members began to exhibit all the symptoms of discouragement and feeling that they could not achieve their goal. At this point, a leader was assigned to the team. He soon recognized that his first priority was to help the team overcome its sense of failure and helplessness. He took the following steps.

First, he had the team take stock of its strengths and weaknesses. It became immediately apparent that the team did not have performance goals which were sufficiently concrete to have a common meaning among all members. The goal with which they had started, as well as the new one that they had defined for themselves, was too general to provide direction.

The team had no way to determine how it was progressing, and members wasted a good deal of time arguing about what the team should be doing. Because it had no clear performance goals, it had no clear plan or strategies for achieving the goals. It was also apparent that the team had not developed the necessary skills and discipline for conducting effective and efficient meetings. Faced with the obvious facts of their own failure, team members now felt that they had been given an impossible task and that no matter what they did they could not succeed. They had not accepted responsibility for their performance. All the various seeds for failure were rooted in the team's failure to undertake a systematic assessment of its performance. Because the team did not regularly take stock of its performance, it had imperceptibly moved from its initial days of enthusiasm and positive expectations to its present lack of enthusiasm and negative expectations.

Second, the new leader, functioning as a coach, began to help the team find courage and new confidence by translating its assessment of itself into a few concrete and achievable actions. The first thing was to help the team describe a performance goal or set of goals that everyone could understand, which the team could achieve, and against which it could measure its progress. Instead of the vague goals which the team had initially tried to use, the coach helped the team develop the following concrete performance goal: 'to describe the specific steps that the department must take in order to determine the cost-effectiveness of training the department delivers'.

Finally, once the team had a goal, the coach was able to function as a resource and inject new ideas and approaches into the way the team worked. He suggested that the team do such things as: visit other healthcare organizations and find out how they assessed the value of their training; contact professional training societies and explore databases and other sources of information related to the evaluation of training; and interview the people who used their training to find out how they assessed the training for themselves.

Teams get stuck and become discouraged. For a coach to lift teams out of their discouragement he or she needs to understand how teams often create the seeds for their own discouragement and what kinds of practical help can be given to help teams work their way out of it.

REWARDING

Teams, like individuals, need to feel appreciated in order to try always to do their best. Coaching teams requires that coaches remain sensitive to every opportunity to acknowledge a team's achievement and that they look for creative ways to acknowledge it.

Whenever an organization moves to a team-centred structure, all of the traditional personnel systems must be changed to focus on teams, rather than individuals, as the primary units of production. Among the systems that must be changed is the reward system. What we now find in team-centred organizations is that:

O   There are ways for team members to acknowledge the performance of other team members.

O   There are ways for teams to acknowledge the performance of other teams.

O   Team leaders are given special budgets for recognizing special team achievements with lunches, short trips and other such outings.

O   Skill-based pay is given a team basis, so that no one member can receive extra pay for extra skills until all team members demonstrate competencies in these skills.

O   There are team bonuses based on the performance of teams against previously established performance objectives.

Successful coaches will use all of the ways for rewarding teams that have been established in the larger organization but, in addition, will make extensive use of informal strategies for rewarding team performance. Here are some of the occasions in a team's life when a coach can make sure that its performance and achievements is acknowledged:

O   when a significant project milestone is reached

O   when some significant improvement has been made in a work process

O   when the team has achieved significant cost savings or cost avoidance

O   when the team has resolved a particularly difficult problem

O   when the team has received a particularly good evaluation from its customers

○   when the team has produced innovative ideas for new products or services

○   when the team has achieved some goal or performed some task under cost and earlier than scheduled

○   when the team has responded positively and effectively to some change, such as reorganization, changes in its purpose, changes in team membership or leadership, changes in business goals and budgets and the like

○   when the team has been given some 'thankless' task to perform and accomplishes it with style and without complaint.

INSTRUCTING

As a tool for instructing teams we can use the same Learning Cycle (Figure 5.1, p. 115) for instructing individuals. The principal differences between teaching a team and teaching an individual some new knowledge or skill do not occur in the sequence of instructing. The sequence of proposing what is to be learned and how it will be learned, modelling what is to be learned, and testing if learning has occurred is the same for teams and individuals. The special characteristics of teaching a team exist because:

○   it is the whole team which must learn together and

○   the knowledge and skills that are learned must be employed by the whole team, working together as a team.

These special characteristics may be illustrated by an example. Suppose the coach is teaching the team how to improve a work process and intends that the team be able to use the following steps:

1.   Identify the candidate processes.
2.   Select the process or portion of the process.
3.   Chart the process.
4.   Identify redundancies and other non-value-added candidates for elimination.
5.   Select the appropriate measurements of process performance.
6.   Develop baseline metrics.
7.   Select improvement opportunities.

8.   Make improvements.
9.   Measure and compare to baseline.

For the whole team to learn together means that every member of the team must be involved in the learning process. The way to achieve this is to structure the instruction process so that the team members are fully involved with each other, questioning each other, teaching each other and testing each other's understanding. The pattern for doing this is:

1.   to present and model what is to be learned; and
2.   to turn the learning process over to the team and have the team clarify what has been presented in order to make sure that all team members have learned what has been presented.

Not only should the whole team be involved in the process of instruction, it should also, collectively, demonstrate what has been learned. It may be that the team will decide to assign special responsibilities to individual team members, but improving a team's work process, for example, requires that everyone using the process be involved in its improvement. The coach instructing a team in these steps will structure the process so that all team members demonstrate their competency to work together and apply the steps for improving the work process.

SOLVING PROBLEMS

Successful team coaches are able to help teams solve problems. The process for interacting with a team to solve a problem is no different from that already outlined in Figure 5.2, Solving Problems (see p. 119). However, there are two special characteristics that apply to solving problems with teams. First, the coach is carrying on a conversation with more than one person, is responding to each person, but is also helping members to interact with each other and, through this interaction, to become an important resource for solving a problem. The coach, therefore, is not using the resources of a single person, as when helping an individual solve a problem, but, as in the case of instructing a team, is using the resources of a number of people. The coach's job, then, is to stimulate and manage the interaction among team members, as well as his or her own interaction with each individual.

The second special characteristic of coaching teams to solve problems is that the coach may introduce a special structured process to help the team. Teams require special tools for efficient and effective problem-solving. They need tools which take advantage of all the team's resources and structure the inter-action of team members so that all members are involved. Team coaches must therefore have a second set of special knowledge and skills related to team problem-solving. At the very minimum, a team coach should know how to instruct a team in the use of such basic tools as brainstorming, nominal group technique, fishbone diagrams and so on. All these are covered in detail in 'Special Team Problem-Solving Tools', pp. 149–151.

CHALLENGING

The best teams are challenged teams (Kinlaw, 1991a). Being challenged to produce superior results against significant odds is a fundamental dynamic for creating and maintaining superior teams. Successful coaches understand this, and make sure that their teams are never allowed to become complacent about their achievements, but are continually presented with new opportunities for improvement and to accept different and more difficult responsibilities.

Challenging performance goals and opportunities are some of the primary reasons for forming teams. In today's competitive environment and global economy, the challenges presented to an organization change and multiply with ever-increasing speed. Moving to a team-centred organizational structure has been one of the fundamental strategies for responding to these challenges.

Although organizations certainly form teams to respond to significant performance challenges, it is a mistake to think that the inevitable sequence is: (1) a challenge is recognized; and (2) a team is formed. Performance teams can exist in an unlimited number of shapes and forms. There are natural work groups, project teams, quality improvement teams, customer service teams, process improvement teams, management teams and cross-functional teams, to name just a few. At least some of these teams will have been created by the routine demands of daily production and service rather than by some specific challenge.

Whatever the team and whatever the reasons for its existence, they share one common factor. For these teams to develop and continue as fully integrated and superior performing units, they must have significant performance challenges. Without challenges, teams degenerate into various kinds of groups and collections of people.

Regardless of the kind of team or the reasons for its formation, every team can be presented with the challenge of continuous improvement in the following areas:

○   customer satisfaction
○   work processes
○   input and supplier performance
○   teamwork and team development, and
○   use of human resources.

These winning outcomes are, of course, listed in the Successful Coaching Model (Figure 3.1, p. 34). Teams, however, will face special challenges, such as major loss of market share, product obsolescence, drops in quality, customer complaints, excessive overheads, innovations by competitors and the like. But every performance team, whether it be a natural longstanding work group or a new team created to solve a particular problem, can be challenged to improve all of its winning outcomes.

Some years ago I worked with an engineering firm to create special process improvement teams and to develop existing work groups into teams. One of the first challenges was for the teams to develop themselves into fully functioning teams. I introduced a set of variables – results, work processes, leadership, and team member feelings – which each team used to measure its development. Once each team had developed its own baseline, it used the data to identify improvement opportunities to work on for the following three months. At the end of the three-month period the teams reassessed themselves and compared the new data to their baseline data. They then used the comparisons to monitor their progress and identify new improvement opportunities.

As the training of the teams continued and they continued to monitor their progress, some of the teams began to report that they were assessing themselves at the top of the scales for all four variables. One conclusion might have been that the teams had now reached the peak of team development. The conclusion that we encouraged was that the teams should set new standards for their development and look for new variables to measure that related more directly to their *performance* as teams and not as their *development* as teams. The logic here was:

1. the more mature a team becomes the more it will shift from focusing on its own development to focusing on performance goals and outcomes; and

2. it is challenging outcomes which will have a profound effect on team development.

IMPROVING PERFORMANCE

Improving the performance of teams refers to that coaching application in which the coach confronts the team about performance which is below previously established expectations. All that I have written about improving the performance of individuals in Chapter 5 applies to improving the performance of teams. However, there are two special characteristics that apply to improving the performance of teams. First, the coach is confronting the whole team about its performance and can expect all of the members of the team to respond. Second, during the response that members make and during every step in the process, the coach must help members interact with each other and become, through this interaction, a major resource for understanding the performance problem and for planning how to resolve it. The coach's job is to stimulate and manage the interaction among team members and to involve them in the whole process. When we take this idea of involvement and apply it to the four episodes in a coaching interaction to improve the performance of a team, we get the kinds of coaching behaviour described below.

○ **Initiating.** The coach might start by saying something like 'Thanks for getting together with me. I want to discuss what I see as a problem that is developing and determine what we need to do to fix it'.

○ **Structuring.** The coach might structure the conversation by saying something like 'I want to tell you what I see as a problem, get everyone's reaction to what I see, develop an understanding that we can all agree on, and then put our heads together and find a solution'.

○ **Developing.** During this episode the coach encourages each member to test his or her perceptions with all the other team members. The goal is to develop a body of information which is produced by the full participation of all members and which can be accepted by the coach and all members. Once the problem has been understood and defined to everyone's satisfaction, the coach involves all members in developing solution strategies and follow-up plans to track progress.

○ **Concluding.** The job of the coach here is the same as when improving the performance of individuals. The coach reviews the agreements that have been made and conveys support to the team in helping the team remedy the problem.

 ## SPECIAL TEAM PROBLEM-SOLVING TOOLS

Teams make decisions as teams and they solve problems as teams. There is a large number of problem-solving tools which have been designed specifically for team use and require the interaction and full use of each person present at a team meeting. The third set of special knowledge and skills needed by a successful team coach is a knowledge of how to use these special team problem-solving tools. These tools can be categorized into three groups:
1. generating information and ideas
2. making decisions and evaluating alternatives
3. quality improvement tools.

It is beyond the scope of this book to describe even a portion of the many tools that are available and which have proven utility. I have chosen to give a full description of one tool for each of the first two categories. The third category, quality improvement tools, is a special topic and includes such tools as: data acquisition and analysis, cause-and-effect diagrams, flowcharting, Pareto charts, statistical process control charts and others. Anyone interested in extending their knowledge about team problem-solving tools will find a number of references in the 'Reference and Further Reading' section at the end of this book.

BRAINSTORMING

Brainstorming is a team tool for generating information that involves the spontaneous contribution of ideas from all group members. It requires the use of a flipchart or blackboard to display information generated by the team.

Steps

1. Clarify the ground rules for brainstorming.
2. Define the topic or information target.
3. Go round each member of the group in sequence and request ideas.
4. Record all the ideas.
5. End with input in any order from group members.
6. Review all ideas and clarify – do not eliminate, only reword as needed.
7. Review all ideas and combine ideas that are redundant.
8. Review, clarify and add to develop final list.

Note: Follow these rules when generating ideas:

○ one idea at a time
○ no criticism or discussion
○ record all ideas, even if they seem repetitious
○ let fresh ideas multiply from original ideas.

PRIORITY ANALYSIS

This tool is designed to help a group make a decision, such as selecting the problem or opportunity that it wants to work on, or selecting the strategy that it wants to pursue to solve a problem or take advantage of some new opportunity. It requires the group to develop a list of selection criteria and then assign a ranking to each.

Steps:

1. Give each group member a copy of the Priority Analysis Sheet (Figure 6.1).
2. Review the Priority Analysis Sheet. The analysis criteria are typical, but arbitrary. The group can develop its own, modify what is shown, or use the criteria as shown. Note that, for each criterion, a scale is used to show to what degree the criterion is met by the alternative listed in the first column.
3. List the alternatives under consideration. If the group is trying to decide what problem it wants to work on, list these problems. If the group is working on opportunities (new initiatives, quality improvements, new products) list these. If the group is already working on a problem or opportunity, then list the possible strategies that it may use in the left-hand column.
4. List the alternatives in the first column, then evaluate each alternative using the scale appropriate to each criterion.
5. Once the alternatives have been rated, sum the ratings and enter the total for each alternative in the last column.

Eliminate the alternatives with the lowest scores. Make a final decision between the top one or two by discussion or by repeating the process.

CONCLUSION

In this chapter I have related the function of coaching to the special needs of teams. At the outset I emphasized that coaching teams requires the same fundamental knowledge and

Alternatives (Problems, Opportunities)	Criteria						
	Impor- tance	Resources	Return on Invest- ment	Degree of Difficulty	Approval	Group Capability	Time to Undertake
	5-Critical 4- 3- 2- 1-Not Critical	5-Great 4- 3- 2- 1-Little	5-Great 4- 3- 2- 1-Little	5-Hard 4- 3- 2- 1-Easy	5-None 4- 3- 2- 1-Several Layers	5-Can Do Now 4- 3- 2- 1-Can't Do Now	5-Few Weeks 4- 3- 2- 1-A Year

Figure 6.1 Priority Analysis Sheet (suggested criteria to select a problem/opportunity)

skills as those needed to coach individuals. In addition to these fundamental skills, however, I have identified and described three sets of knowledge and skills that are required for the successful coaching of teams. These were:

1. knowledge and skills for helping a team manage its meetings
2. knowledge and skills for using the coaching applications with teams – that is, giving feedback, encouraging, rewarding, instructing, solving problems, challenging, and improving performance
3. knowledge and skills for using special team problem-solving tools.

I have now covered all the information that a person requires for being a successful coach of winning individuals and winning teams. In Chapter 7, I will describe the strategies that anyone who wants to become a successful coach can use.

CHAPTER

7

BECOMING A SUCCESSFUL COACH

This final chapter fulfils the primary purpose of this book, which has been to provide the reader with the necessary understanding and tools for becoming a successful coach. Here, I will show how the material presented in the previous chapters can be used as a practical resource for anyone who wants to become a successful coach.

DEVELOPMENTAL STRATEGIES

What are some of the important strategies that a person can use to become a successful coach? What are the specific sources of help? What are the guidelines for action? In this section I will describe briefly a set of strategies which, in my experience, constitute ways for developing oneself as a coach. In subsequent sections, I will describe each of these strategies in detail and provide a number of suggestions for action. The strategies use:

○   the Successful Coaching Model
○   personal assessment
○   practice
○   feedback and
○   preparation.

USING THE SUCCESSFUL COACHING MODEL

The framework for learning, practising and assessing our development as a coach is the Successful Coaching Model (Figure 3.1, p. 34). The Model is the primary source of information about coaching and it identifies the specific elements which contribute to the development of a successful coach. The first, and most important, action that we can take to develop as a coach is to become thoroughly familiar with the Model. Particular attention should be given to the coaching interaction and its elements described in the Model. It is the interaction between a coach and individuals or teams which determines the degree to which instrumental results and winning outcomes are achieved.

PERSONAL ASSESSMENT

We can proceed into the future most confidently if we know where we are in the present. It is not always possible to be as accurate as we might hope when taking stock of our own competencies, but it is still a useful task. The kind of tools that we use to assess our performance as a coach have a great deal to do with the accuracy and utility of the information that we generate. When I come to discuss personal assessment below, I will provide a tool that has proven value in helping people develop useful information about their development and performance as coaches. This tool is the *Coaching Competencies Questionnaire*.

PRACTICE

Very often, at the end of the many workshops on coaching that I have led, the participants have asked questions about next steps and what they might do to continue to improve their coaching skills. One way that I have responded is to say: 'There are two rules for becoming a successful coach. The first rule is practice. The second rule is, see rule one.'

Because coaching is largely a communication process, it demands the skilled use of very specific communication behaviours. But it also requires more – it requires that these behaviours be used to create and develop a logical process.

FEEDBACK

Another developmental support that we can use to increase our coaching competencies is feedback. Because coaching obviously is always undertaken with other people, it is those whom we coach who are most able to tell us how well we do the job. Feedback may be obtained during a practice session which we have designed with colleagues, or from the people whom we actually coach – both individuals and teams. When I come to describe below how to organize and use feedback, I will discuss the use of feedback under both conditions.

PREPARATION

Another way in which we can develop as a coach is to take the time to prepare for a coaching interaction, when there is the time and opportunity. While many coaching interactions are, as I have described earlier, unplanned and spontaneous, many other coaching interactions that are scheduled events – for example, a co-worker might ask to see us to discuss some problem, or we might plan a session to teach a co-worker some new skill, or we schedule a time to resolve a perceived performance problem. On such occasions, there are a number of preparations that a coach can make for the interaction and to help ensure its success.

 ## USING THE SUCCESSFUL COACHING MODEL

In Chapter 3, where I described the uses of the Successful Coaching Model, I indicated that one of its uses was to 'provide us with a framework for undertaking our own development as successful coaches' (p. 33). The Model provides us with a framework in that:

○   it reminds us, at all times, that the purpose of coaching is to produce winning performance outcomes

○   identifies the specific, instrumental results that lead to winning outcomes

○   emphasizes the foundational position of the coaching interaction as the source of winning outcomes

○   identifies the specific elements that a coach must manage in order to conduct a successful coaching interaction.

The goal is for the Model to become the consistent way that we think about coaching and that it always remains at the back of our mind whenever we undertake a coaching interaction. For this to happen we must translate the Model into our own words and be able to communicate the model to others. Suggested below are a few ways of integrating the Model into our routine thinking and behaviour:

1.   Over a period of a few weeks, reread Chapter 3 and underscore those things which you think are of particular importance to you.

2.   Practise describing for yourself, in your own words, the information communicated in the Model.

3.   Practise drawing the Model, elaborating on each of the elements as you place them in the Model.

4.   Communicate the Model to some of your colleagues, and test your ability to respond to their questions.

 ## USING PERSONAL ASSESSMENT

One way to monitor your progress as a coach is to assess yourself on the degree to which you have incorporated into your thinking and behaviour the key elements that contribute to successful coaching. One tool for doing this is the *Coaching Competencies Questionnaire* (Figure 7.1, pp. 159–161).

There are four columns after each item in the questionnaire. In the first column indicate whether you think that you are

Coaching Competencies Questionnaire: Self				
	Doing OK	Need to Improve	Data	Planned Action
In my relationships with my co-workers:				
1. I show them I believe they want to be fully competent in their jobs.				
2. I give them the complete opportunity to demonstrate their competence.				
3. I regularly express to them my confidence in their capacity to succeed.				
4. I make minimum use of direct controls (such as direct oversight and status reports) in managing their performance.				
5. I never blame them when they present performance problems.				
6. I give them every opportunity to improve when they make mistakes.				
7. I ensure that their work is as challenging as I can make it.				
8. I am readily available to talk to about improving performance.				
9. I make it easy for them to tell me that they don't know how to do something.				
10. I often initiate conversations to help them perform at their best.				
In my coaching conversations with co-workers:				
11. I always make sure that there is full give-and-take.				
12. I always ensure that concrete language is used.				
13. I always ensure that all necessary information is developed before drawing conclusions.				
14. I always ensure that there is shared responsibility for improving performance.				

Figure 7.1 The Coaching Competencies Questionnaire (continued)

	Doing OK	Need to Improve	Data	Planned Action
15. I always ensure that conversations move forward in a logical manner.				
16. I always clarify the purposes of every conversation.				
17. I always help these conversations stay focused.				
18. I always take into account the feelings of others.				
19. I never make them feel inferior.				
20. I always develop mutual understanding in searching for solutions to problems.				
21. I always give full attention to what they are saying.				
22. I am never quick to reject what they are trying to communicate.				
23. I rarely interrupt them when they are speaking.				
24. I rarely give them irrelevant information.				
25. I always help them provide information needed to reach the goal of the conversation.				
26. I respond quickly to let them know when I have understood what they are saying.				
27. I always fully use the other person's knowledge and understanding of the topic.				
28. I always help them clarify their own understanding of problems.				
29. I always make it easy for them to disagree with me.				
30. I always express appreciation for their willingness to resolve the problems being discussed.				
I regularly find coaching opportunities to:				
31. Give co-workers constructive feedback on their performance.				
32. Help co-workers find alternatives when their performance seems blocked.				

Figure 7.1 Continued

	Doing OK	Need to Improve	Data	Planned Action
33. Express appreciation for the performance of co-workers.				
34. Share my own competencies with co-workers.				
35. Help co-workers solve problems that block their performance.				
36. Encourage co-workers to find the solutions to their own performance problems.				
37. Give co-workers the opportunity to try more and more difficult tasks.				
38. Express confidence in what co-workers are doing.				
I am quick to:				
39. Improve unsatisfactory performance.				
40. Help co-workers cope with failure.				

Figure 7.1 Concluded

'Doing OK' at that item. Avoid as far as possible the tendency to be too generous in evaluating your competencies. In the third column, headed 'Data', write down the proof or support of your assessment – in other words, validate your assessment.

If you judge that you need to improve at a competency put a tick in the second column and note in the 'Data' column what you are doing or not doing that suggests you might improve. In the fourth column, headed 'Planned Action', note what you plan to do to improve.

The Coaching Competencies Questionnaire (CCQ) contains 40 items and measures the degree to which a person demonstrates the following characteristics in his or her performance:
1. commitment to the *beliefs* of successful coaches (items 1–10);
2. competencies to create the *qualities* of successful coaching interactions (items 11–20);

3.   competencies in the *core skills* required to conduct successful coaching interactions (items 21–30); and

4.   competencies to use coaching in a full range of *applications* (items 31–40).

After you have completed the CCQ for the first time, record your improvement actions. Put your completed CCQ away for later use, and get on with your improvement actions. After three months or so, complete the CCQ again, without referring to your initial assessment. Compare the first completed CCQ with the second. Record your improvements and your new improvement actions.

The CCQ can be used as an ongoing resource for improving coaching performance. You can reassess yourself any time you feel the need or use the CCQ in a less formal way and simply run through the items periodically to remind yourself of what you should be doing to be a successful coach.

When I come to discuss feedback, I will show how the CCQ can be used to obtain feedback from our co-workers. When we use the CCQ in this way we not only discover our own perceptions of ourselves, we are also able to compare this perception with the way others see us.

The CCQ can be modified to obtain an assessment of your coaching skills from your co-workers. Figure 7.2 shows how you might modify the CCQ to use in this way. Only the first ten items are modified as an illustration.

 PRACTICE

Coaching is a skilled interaction, and the development of coaching skills (like the development of any other kind of skills) requires practice. In this section I will concentrate on three of the elements that must be integrated for a successful coaching interaction. These elements, previously described in Chapter 4, are: the *qualities* of a successful interaction; the *core skills* required to create a successful interaction; and the *process* that

**Coaching Competencies Questionnaire: Other
Instructions**

For each item in the CCQ, there is a scale of possible responses from 5 to 1. For each of the items, indicate the degree to which the item accurately describes the person you are rating by circling the appropriate number. If you circle '5', you are indicating that the behaviour or performance described in the item is 'very characteristic' of the person you are rating. If you circle a '1', you are indicating that the behaviour is 'very uncharacteristic' of the person. By circling 2, 3 or 4, you are indicating that your assessment lies between the extremes of 5 and 1. Please complete **every** item, and return it in the envelope provided to the person who gave it to you.

To what degree do you believe that the following statements are characteristic of the person you are rating? Circle the number that you believe applies to the person for each statement.

5	4	3	2	1
Very Characteristic	Moderately Characteristic	Somewhat Characteristic	Moderately Uncharacteristic	Very Uncharacteristic

In his/her relationships with his/her co-workers, he/she:

1. Shows them he/she believes they want to be fully competent in their jobs. 5 4 3 2 1
2. Gives them the complete opportunity to demonstrate their competence. 5 4 3 2 1
3. Regularly expresses to them his/her confidence in their capacity to succeed. 5 4 3 2 1
4. Makes minimum use of controls (such as direct oversight and status reports) in managing their performance. 5 4 3 2 1
5. Never blames them when they present performance problems. 5 4 3 2 1
6. Gives them every opportunity to improve when they make mistakes. 5 4 3 2 1
7. Ensures that their work is as challenging as he/she can make it. 5 4 3 2 1
8. Is readily available to talk to about improving performance. 5 4 3 2 1
9. Makes it easy for them to tell him/her they don't know how to do something. 5 4 3 2 1
10. Often initiates conversations to help them perform at their full potential. 5 4 3 2 1

Figure 7.2 Modification of the CCQ

underlies a successful interaction. I have not included the fourth element, *beliefs*, as one which we can strengthen directly by practice. Our belief in the value and importance of coaching will be strengthened through our success as coaches. The first ten questions of the *Coaching Competencies Questionnaire (CCQ)* help us assess the degree to which our beliefs about coaching are revealed by our behaviour, and we can use the CCQ to monitor our beliefs about coaching.

The way to develop our competencies in the qualities of successful coaching, the core skills and the process can be separated into the following steps:

O   **Step 1.** Understand the qualities of a successful coaching interaction.
O   **Step 2.** Understand each core skill and practise it separately.
O   **Step 3.** Practise integrating your understanding and use of several skills.
O   **Step 4.** Understand the core process of coaching.
O   **Step 5.** Understand and practise using the core process with the applications of coaching.

STEP 1: UNDERSTAND THE QUALITIES OF A SUCCESSFUL COACHING INTERACTION

The essential qualities which must be present in a successful coaching interaction are:

O   respect
O   mutuality
O   concreteness, and
O   trust.

An important step towards becoming a successful coach is to understand each of these qualities and to know what we do and what we don't do to create these qualities.

Respect

Do the following to make sure that you understand how to create *respect*:

1.   Review the meaning of *respect* in Chapter 4 (pp. 75–76) and then do the following exercises:

○   Recall a conversation that you have had with another co-worker in which you did not feel respected. List what the co-worker did that made you feel that you were not being respected.

○   Recall a conversation that you have had with another co-worker in which you felt fully respected. List what the co-worker did that made you feel that you were being fully respected.

○   Imagine that you are having a coaching session to teach a co-worker some new knowledge or skill. What might you say at the beginning of the session to put him or her at ease and to show full respect for the co-worker's willingness and capacity to learn?

2.   Start observing co-workers' interactions around you. What do you notice when respect is being fully communicated and when it is not?

Mutuality

Do the following to make sure that you understand how to create *mutuality*:

1.   Review the meaning of *mutuality* found in Chapter 4 (pp. 77–78) and then do the following exercises:

○   Describe three meanings of mutuality.

○   Describe how mutuality differs from equal participation in a coaching interaction.

○   Describe the meaning of shared responsibility in a coaching interaction.

2.   Start observing co-workers' interactions around you. What do you notice when conversations are fully mutual and when they are not? Notice the behaviour of co-workers when they are not fully included in a conversation.

Concreteness

Do the following to ensure that you understand how to create *concreteness*:

1.   Review the meaning of *concreteness* found in Chapter 4 (pp. 78–79) and then answer the following questions:

○   What is the effect of coaching communication that is not concrete?

○   What can you do to ensure that your coaching language is concrete?

2.   Turn each of the statements below into ones which are more concrete:

   ○   **Statement:** 'You're doing a fine job.'
   ○   **Statement:** 'You weren't very helpful during our team meeting yesterday.'
   ○   **Statement:** 'We really want to do a professional job on this paper.'

Trust

Do the following to ensure that you understand how to create *trust*:

1.   Review the meaning of *trust* found in Chapter 4 (pp. 79–83) and then answer the following questions:

   ○   How are the other essential qualities in a coaching interaction related to trust?
   ○   Explain how trust is a function of accurate information held by both coach and the persons being coached.

2.   Review Figure 4.1, 'Trust as a function of knowing' (p. 80) and answer the following questions:

   ○   What are the characteristics of the four quadrants in Figure 4.1?
   ○   What can a coach do to enlarge Quadrant A – that is, 'both coach and persons coached have accurate information'?
   ○   What behaviours might coaches use which keep them from creating a fully developed Quadrant A?

STEP 2: UNDERSTAND EACH CORE SKILL AND PRACTISE IT SEPARATELY

There are three sets of core coaching skills:
○   communicating attention
○   developing information, and
○   conveying support and confidence.

To practise these skills we must first understand them so thoroughly that we need never question ourselves as to whether we are using them well or badly. The second step in practising these skills is to use them. For each of the three sets of skills, you will find below a number of actions that you can take to: (1) test your understanding of these skills, and (2) practise the use of the skills.

Understanding and practising communicating attention

The first set of core skills is communicating attention. This set of skills is important during each of the four episodes of a coaching interaction. There are two behavioural elements in paying attention and conveying to others that you are paying attention. These elements are: listening and observing and testing. In this section you will first find some suggestions for making sure that you understand the exact meaning of paying attention and then some practice activities for learning to use this set of skills. Learning to use the skill of *reflecting* is of particular importance.

Do the following to ensure that you understand *listening and observing*:

1.   Review the meaning of *listening and observing* found in Chapter 4 (pp. 85–86) and then answer the following questions:
     O   What are the reasons that often keep us from listening well?
     O   What are some of the clues in our own behaviour that we are not listening well?
2.   List the behaviours which successful coaches use to listen and convey that they are listening.

Do the following to practise the skills of *listening and observing*:

1.   At the next social interaction that you have at home or with friends, concentrate on using the behaviours of listening and observing – that is:
     O   face the other people
     O   maintain good eye contact
     O   express your involvement using your face and body
     O   acknowledge what other people are saying with such vocal expressions as 'Uh huh', 'Right', 'Great', 'OK', and the like
     O   don't interrupt.

2.   As you practise your listening skills, notice the impact that your use of good listening skills has on other people.

3.   As you are listening to other people, pay attention to their non-verbal communication. What are they saying with their bodies and their tone of voice?

Do the following to ensure that you understand *reflecting* as a skill for *testing* your understanding of what others are saying:

1.   Review the meaning of testing and the specific skill of reflecting in Chapter 4 (pp. 86–88).

2.   Write out the ways that you might begin a reflecting response – for example, 'So it seems to you . . . '

Do the following to practise the skill of *reflecting*:

1.   Imagine that the following statements have been made to you. Write out a reflecting response for each statement. Compare your responses to the ones on p. 87 in Chapter 4. Your responses will not be the same, but use the example responses to judge whether your responses are true reflecting responses.

    O   **Statement:** 'No matter what I do or how loud I complain, I am having no luck getting the cooperation that I need from drafting.'

    O   **Statement:** 'We are spending so much time getting our team organized to respond to our customers that there isn't much time left to respond to them. Management wants us to keep our customers completely happy and still spend all this extra time learning to work differently. We are the ones caught right in the middle.'

    O   **Statement:** 'All my group seems to get from top management is a lot of negative stuff. We get blamed, even when we shouldn't be. When anyone complains about our services, management just assumes that we are in the wrong.'

2.   At the next social interaction that you have at home or with friends, concentrate on using some reflecting responses during your conversations. Pay attention to what other people do when you use a reflecting response. You should find that they continue to expand and elaborate whatever they are describing.

3. Watch a programme on television in which one person is interviewing another. Then:
    ○   notice whether the interviewer uses reflecting responses
    ○   formulate your own reflecting responses to what the interviewee says

Understanding and practising developing information

The episodes of a coaching interaction in sequence are initiating and structuring: it is during the third episode, developing, that the following skills have particular value:
○   probing
○   summarizing, and
○   connecting.

Probing

Do the following to ensure that you understand *probing* as a skill for *developing information*:

1. Review the description of *probing* in Chapter 4 (p. 89), then answer the following questions:
    ○   What are the purposes of a probing response?
    ○   What is the difference between a closed probe and an open probe?
    ○   What is the general effect of a closed probe? Of an open probe?

Do the following to practise the skill of *probing* as a skill for *developing information*:

1. Which of the following probes are closed and which are open?
    ○   'Did you accept the challenge?'
    ○   'How much time do you require?'
    ○   'Tell me how you think we should proceed from here.'
    ○   'Give me a description of the resources you need.'
    ○   'Give me the name of the contractor.'
    ○   'Tell me what time you arrived at the meeting.'
    ○   'What sort of plan do you have for getting the project on track?'
    ○   'What can we do to decrease our costs as soon as possible?'

2. Write out a closed and an open probe as a response to each of the following statements:
    ○   **Statement:** 'There was not time to do all the things that we wanted to do to get ready for the presentation. We were just not given enough lead time.'
    ○   **Statement:** 'It is difficult to know what next steps we should take to keep the team members enthusiastic and wanting to learn more about working together. We seem to have hit a brick wall.'
    ○   **Statement:** 'I have a lot of trouble advising our new employees what to expect and how to take care of themselves. With our history of downsizing, no one believes that the company is going to look after its employees.
3. At the next social interaction that you have at home or with friends, concentrate on using probing behaviours and observe the effect.

Summarizing
Do the following to ensure that you understand *summarizing* as a skill for *developing information*:
1. Review the description of *summarizing* as a skill for *developing information* in Chapter 4 (pp. 89–91), then answer the following questions:
    ○   What is a summarizing statement?
    ○   When might you use a summarizing statement?
    ○   What does a summarizing statement accomplish?
2. During your next small group or team meeting, notice when a summarizing statement is made and how it affects the group's interaction.
    Do the following to practise the skill of *summarizing* as a skill for *developing information*:
1. Listen to some portion of a news broadcast or presentation on the radio or television. Turn off the radio or television and summarize what you have heard.
2. At the next social interaction that you have at home or with friends, concentrate on using one or two summarizing responses and observe the effect.

3. Read two or three pages of a book and then summarize what you have read.
4. During the next team meeting or small group meeting that you attend, summarize at least once what the team or group has been talking about.

Connecting
Do the following to ensure that you understand *connecting* as a skill for *developing information*:
1. Review the description of *connecting* as a skill for *developing information* in Chapter 4 (pp. 89–91), then answer the following questions:
    ○ What is the purpose of a connecting response?
    ○ What kinds of connection might a coach make to help others develop greater clarity about the topic they are discussing?
2. During your next small group or team meeting, notice when a connecting statement is made and how it affects the group's interaction.

Do the following to practise the skill of *connecting* as a skill for *developing information*:
1. Observe or listen to an interview being conducted on the radio or television. Identify when the interviewer makes a connecting statement.
2. Observe or listen to an interview being conducted on the radio or television. Listen for opportunities to make a connecting statement and make it.

Understanding and practising conveying support and confidence

Two kinds of skills have particular value during the final stage of a coaching interaction, concluding. During this final episode, the coach *confirms* what has been accomplished, by summarizing what has been accomplished, by reviewing the plan of action the people being coached will follow after the coaching interaction, testing for final agreement and testing to ensure mutual agreement on what transpired during the coaching interaction. The coach also *affirms* the potential the other people have for success and conveys confidence in, and continuing support for, them.

Do the following to ensure that you understand *confirming* and *affirming* as skills for concluding a *coaching interaction*:

1.   Review the description of *confirming* in Chapter 4 (pp. 97–98) and answer the following questions:

     ○   What does the coach intend to accomplish by confirming what has transpired in the conversation?

     ○   What does it mean to affirm the person being coached at the end of a transaction?

2.   During your next small group or team meeting, identify any examples of confirming and affirming and their results.

Do the following to practise the skills of *confirming* and *affirming* as skills for concluding a *coaching interaction*:

1.   Review the two concluding statements below and identify those parts which are confirming and which are affirming:

     ○   **Statement:** 'Let's review what we have accomplished and what still needs to be done. We've set out the steps for establishing some benchmarks for our procurement process. We've identified the companies that you will contact in the next ten days. I believe you have a clear grasp of how to develop benchmarks and what you will do next. Is there anything we need to clear up before we end?'

     ○   **Statement:** 'The problem, as we have defined it, is that we have too many changes that our customers want after we think the design has been fixed. What seems to be missing is a clearer up-front definition of what the customer wants, and not enough customer participation in our design review process. What we have agreed to is that you will put together a plan to resolve these two problems and you and I will discuss them on Tuesday. You know the problems, and I have no doubt that your solutions will be right on target. Do you have any questions?'

STEP 3: PRACTISE INTEGRATING YOUR UNDERSTANDING AND THE USE OF SEVERAL SKILLS

Now that you have worked at understanding the qualities of a successful coaching interaction and the skills, the next step is to practise using several of the skills at the same time. Here are some suggestions for integrating your understanding and the use of several skills at once.

1. Select a social opportunity when you will be having casual conversations with your friends or family. Set yourself the task of practising the three skills of listening and observing, reflecting and probing. When you are employing a skill, mentally label it.
2. Select a social opportunity when you will be having casual conversations with your friends or family. Set yourself the task of practising the two skills of summarizing and connecting. When you are employing a skill, mentally label it.
3. Select a social opportunity when you will be having casual conversations with your friends or family. Set for yourself the task of practising all the skills of listening and observing, reflecting, probing, summarizing and connecting. When you are employing a skill, mentally label it.
4. Select a small group or team meeting which you will attend. Take into the meeting a list of the skills that you will consciously use. Each time you use the skill, put a tick by the skill on your list.

STEP 4: UNDERSTAND THE CORE PROCESS OF COACHING

Underlying all successful coaching is a logical process that flows through four episodes. Developing ourselves into successful coaches requires that we are able to use the qualities and skills, covered above, and build the process. The next step in our development is to understand the core process. Here are some actions that you can take.

1. Review the description of the core process in Chapter 4 (pp. 92–94). Pay particular attention to Figure 4.2, 'The coaching process' (p. 93). Answer the following questions:

○   What is a process as applied to a coaching interaction?
○   Describe the four episodes in a coaching interaction.
2.   The following are not very useful ways to initiate a coaching conversation. Change the statements into more useful ones:

○   **Statement:** 'You should have picked up how to process those problem reports from your colleagues, but it looks like I will now have to spend time showing you how.'

○   **Statement:** 'I'm on a tight schedule and I want to get this over as quickly as we can. You've been doing pretty much the same thing for too long, and I want to move you to another job that will get your brain cells working again.'

3.   The second episode in a coaching interaction is structuring. Imagine that you are structuring a coaching interaction for any of the coaching applications below. What might you say:

○   for giving feedback?
○   for instructing?
○   for challenging?

4.   The third episode in a coaching interaction is developing information. What skills will you concentrate on using to develop information with the people being coached?

5.   The final stage in a coaching interaction is concluding. What are some of the points that you might cover in concluding a coaching interaction to instruct? To solve a problem?

STEP 5: UNDERSTAND AND PRACTISE USING THE CORE PROCESS WITH THE APPLICATIONS OF COACHING

Coaching exists in a number of applications – that is, it produces different kinds of results. The final step in developing ourselves as successful coaches is to understand and practise using the qualities, skills and core process in some specific application. Here are some actions that you can take:

1. Review the descriptions of the coaching applications in Chapter 5 and answer the following:
    O What is the difference between an informal coaching application and a formal application?
    O Describe each of the coaching applications.
    O What are some of the opportunities coaches have for giving feedback?
    O What are the characteristics of useful feedback?
    O What are the three characteristics of encouragement that works?
    O What are some things that coaches can do to increase the power of their rewards?
    O Describe in your own words the teaching/learning cycle found in Figure 5.1.
2. Review Figure 5.2 in Chapter 5 (p. 119) and do the following:
    O List the goals for each episode in an interaction to solve problems.
    O Select a problem that a co-worker has presented to you in the past. Use Figure 5.2 and, for each of the goals in each of the episodes of the process, describe what should happen.
3. Review Figure 5.3 in Chapter 5 (p. 124) and do the following:
    O List the goals for each episode in an interaction to improve performance.
    O Select a conversation that you might have in the future with a co-worker to improve performance. Use Figure 5.3 and, for each of the goals in each of the episodes of the process, describe what should happen.
4. Imagine that you are conducting a coaching interaction to improve performance. In the structuring episode of the interaction, your job is to make a preliminary assertion of the nature of the problem. Describe what the characteristics of this assertion should be.
5. Read over the following asserting statements. Label each of the three characteristics of a good asserting statement as they appear in each of the statements.
    O **Assertion:** 'I think we agreed that you would clear up the backlog of service requests by the first of this month. We have passed the first of

the month and there is still a considerable backlog. We are losing customers because we are not responding to their service requests. This is a problem that we must put right. I want to work with you and figure out how we can eliminate the backlog as quickly as possible.'

○ **Assertion:** 'We seem to still be falling behind our projected schedule for installing the hardwire for our new network system. We are not just losing time – we are running over our projected costs and holding up the people who are coming behind with the new hardware and software installations. According to your last estimate, we are now at least a week behind the last schedule you gave me. Let's put our heads together and do whatever we need to do to get the project back on track.'

6. Imagine that you are conducting a coaching interaction to improve performance. The performance problem is that the co-worker has failed to submit a budget report on time. What might you say in the initiating episode? In the structuring episode?

 ## USING FEEDBACK

Coaching is effective when it is effective with the people coached. Successful coaching exists when winning outcomes are achieved. The best sources of information about how well we coach are the people whom we coach. There are two settings in which we can obtain feedback. We can organize a practice coaching session with a colleague and have the colleague give us feedback or obtain feedback from the people whom we actually coach, both individuals and teams.

FEEDBACK IN PRACTICE COACHING SESSIONS

Here are the steps for organizing a practice session with a colleague. I will use the example of a problem-solving application, but you can use the same process for practising any of the applications. You will need two colleagues to help you – one to present a problem and the other to act as observer. The sequence for a practice session is as follows:

1. Review the feedback sheet with your colleagues.
2. Review the problem-solving process that you are trying to use (Figure 5.2, p. 119) with your colleagues.
3. The first colleague presents a problem and you interact for 10 minutes, functioning as a coach and trying to help the colleague solve the problem. The colleague should preferably present a real problem and not play a role.
4. The second colleague observes and completes the *Feedback Sheet* in Figure 7.3.
5. The second colleague serves as a timekeeper. At the end of 10 minutes, the interaction is stopped and colleague gives feedback, using the *Feedback Sheet.*
6. Based on the feedback, identify ways that you can improve your coaching skills.

If you have a video recorder available, you and one colleague can replay the tape of your practice session to complete the *Feedback Sheet.* If you use a videotape you will need only one colleague to help you.

FEEDBACK IN REAL COACHING SESSIONS

You have two options in obtaining feedback from real coaching sessions. You can indicate to your co-worker before the session that you would like to get feedback at the end of the session, or you can request feedback at the end of the session, without alerting your co-worker that you intend to do so. You can use the same *Feedback Sheet* that you might use in a practice session. You can either ask your co-worker to fill the sheet out, or you can use the sheet to ask your co-worker the questions on the sheet.

Characteristic	Examples of specific behaviours that helped create characteristic	Comments
Respect		
Mutuality		
Concreteness		
Trust		

Skill	Frequency (Listening and observing: note quality)	Comments
Listening and Observing		
Reflecting		
Open Probes		
Closed Probes		
Summarizing		
Connecting		
Confirming		
Affirming		

Figure 7.3 Feedback Sheet (problem-solving application)

■ PREPARATION

The final strategy that I identified at the beginning of this chapter for developing ourselves as coaches is preparation. There are at least three ways that you can prepare for a coaching interaction:
1. Prepare and use job aids.
2. Write out and rehearse the initial words that you plan to say.
3. Mentally image the process as you imagine it should go.

PREPARE AND USE JOB AIDS

A job aid is a written source of information to which you can refer whenever undertaking some particular task. It is a reference that is used in real time – that is, it is used as you carry out the task. When I have been learning to use some new computer software, for instance, I write out the steps for performing the more repetitive functions and keep them in sight until I can perform them automatically, without much conscious thought.

All of the models and figures that I have provided in this book can be used as job aids. Of particular value are 'The Successful Coaching Model' (Figure 3.1), the 'Coaching process' (Figure 4.2), 'Solving problems' (Figure 5.2), and 'Improving performance' (Figure 5.3). You could put copies of these figures on your desk or attach them to a clipboard. In this way, you can refer to them before the coaching session begins, as well as during its progress. You may not need to reproduce the whole figures. For example, you may only need to remind yourself of the four episodes of the coaching process; in this case, just copy out the sequence of initiating, structuring, developing and concluding.

REHEARSE

Another way to prepare for a coaching session, and to help discipline yourself to use the Successful Coaching Model, is to write out the first words that you intend to use at the outset of the session. This is of particular value in the case of improving performance. The beginning of this kind of coaching session is extremely important and is predictive of the success of the whole interaction. The episodes of initiating and structuring are accomplished by what the coach says, and the most important element in these early episodes is how the coach asserts his or her perception of the problem. Write out the assertion and make sure that:

○   it is concrete
○   it describes why the problem is important
○   it makes it clear that you want to solve the problem and not find fault.

IMAGE THE PROCESS

Another way to prepare for a coaching session is to picture in your mind the interchange between yourself and the people being coached. Imagine how you start the session and then how the other person responds, and how you respond to the response.

The process of imaging is particularly valuable when you anticipate that there will be some resistance or negative reaction to the purpose of the session. Remember that negative reactions should never be resisted or fought. They should just be used to develop information. The best skills for responding to negative reactions are reflecting and probing. You might imagine a negative reaction and then how you might respond with a *reflecting* or *probing* behaviour.

 CONCLUSION

I have now described five strategies that you can use to develop yourself as a successful coach:

○   the Successful Coaching Model
○   personal assessment

○   practice
○   feedback, and
○   preparation.
I have also outlined the kind of actions that you can take to use the strategies. All of these strategies and all of these actions depend on a quality that cannot be taught directly through any set of exercises – *your own commitment to become a successful coach*.

Becoming a successful coach is not one of the easiest things to achieve. Coaching is fundamentally an interaction between a coach and other people. One of the most difficult sets of skills to learn is interpersonal communication skills. Learning to be a successful coach requires determination and a long-term view.

Once you start to learn how to be a successful coach, I am confident that your commitment will grow through your successes. Every improvement you make in using the qualities, process and skills that I have outlined will bring you new successes in creating winning individuals and winning teams.

REFERENCES AND FURTHER READING

Anonymous (1994a), 'A hospital's cure for management headaches: an executive coaching case study', *Training and Development Journal*, February, 37.

Anonymous (1994b), 'Levi Strauss & Company implements new pay and performance system', *Employees Benefit Plan Review*, **48**, (7), January, 46–48.

Aurelino, S. and Kennedy, J. (1991), 'Performance coaching: a key to effectiveness', *Supervisory Management*, August, 1–2.

Bass, B.M. (1976), 'Self-managing systems, Z.E.G. and other unthinkables', *Humanizing Organizational Behavior*, H. Meltzer and F. Wickert (eds), Springfield, IL: Charles C. Thomas, 134–155.

Bennis, W. (1995), 'Creating leaders', *Executive Excellence*, October, 5.

Brewer, G. (1995), 'The new managers', *Incentive* (Performance Supplement), March, 30–35.

Boyett, J. and Conn, H. (1991), *Workplace 2000*, New York: Penquin Books USA, Inc.

Chari, W. (1995), 'Why a coach?', *Broker World*, **15**, (7), July, 88–90.

Christmas, B. (1994), 'Coaching vs. managing', *Apparel Industry Magazine*, **55**, (4), April, 70.

Frangos, S. (1993), *Team Zebra*, Essex Junction, VT: Oliver Wright Publications, Inc.

Hankins, C. and Kleiner, B. (1995), 'New developments in supervisor training', *Industrial and Commercial Training*, **27**, (1), 26–32.

Hutcheson, Peggy G. (1996), 'Ten tips for coaches', *Training and Development Journal*, March, 15–16.

Kiechel, W. (1991), 'The boss as coach', *Fortune*, **124**, November, 201.

Kinlaw, D. (1989), *Coaching for Commitment*, San Diego, CA: Pfeiffer & Co.

Kinlaw, D. (1990), *Trainer's Package: Coaching for Commitment*, San Diego, CA: Pfeiffer & Co.

Kinlaw, D. (1991a), *Developing Superior Work Teams*, New York: Lexington Books.

Kinlaw, D. (1991b), *Motivation Assessment Inventory*, Norfolk, VA: Developmental Products.

Kinlaw, D. (1992), *Continuous Improvement and Measurement for Total Quality*, New York: Business One, Irwin.

Kinlaw, D. (1993), *Team Managed Facilitation*, San Diego, CA: Pfeiffer & Co.

Kinlaw, D. (1996a), *The Practice of Empowerment*, Aldershot: Gower.

Kinlaw, D. (1996b), *ASTD Trainer's Sourcebook: Coaching*, New York: McGraw-Hill.

Kinlaw, D. (1996c), *ASTD Trainer's Sourcebook: Facilitation*, New York: McGraw-Hill.

Knippen J. and Green, T. (1990), 'Coaching', *Management Accounting*, May, 36–38.

Koonce, R. (1994), 'One to one', *Training and Development Journal*, February, 34–40.

Koonce, R. (1995), 'Becoming your own career coach', *Training and Development*, January, 18–25.

Luke, R. and Berney, M. (1995), 'Coaching tips from the ballpark', *Training and Development*, February, 7–8.

McNutt, R. and Wright, P. (1995), 'Coaching employees: applying sports analogies to business', *Executive Development*, **8**, (1), 27–32.

Nordhaus-Bike, A. (1995), 'Score one for coaching', *Hospitals and Health Networks*, **69**, (13), July, 5, 41–42.

Orsburn, J., Moran, L., Musselwhite, E. and Zenger, J. (1990), Homewood, IL: Business One, Irwin.

Rao, S. (1994), 'The painful remaking of Ameritech', *Training*, July, 45–53.

Reich, R. B. (1987), 'Entrepreneurship reconsidered: the team as hero', *Harvard Business Review*, May–June, 77–83.

Robertson-Saunders, P. (1991), 'Using feedback to improve performance', *Supervisory Management*, August, 3.

Snyder, A. (1995), 'Executive coaching: the new solution', *Management Review*, **84**, (3), March, 29–32.

Tichy, N. and Charan, R. (1995), 'The CEO as coach: an interview with AlliedSignal's Lawrence A. Bossidy', *Harvard Business Review*, March–April, 69–78.

Wellins, R.S., Byham, W.C. and Dixon, G.R. (1991), *Empowered Teams*, San Francisco: Jossey-Bass.

Wellins, R.S., Byham, W.C. and Dixon, G.R. (1994), *Inside Teams*, San Francisco: Jossey-Bass.

Whetten, D. and Cameron, K. (1991), *Developing Management Skills*, New York: Harper Collins Publishers.

INDEX